OCR CLASSICAL CIVILISATION FOR GCSE

TEACHER'S HANDBOOK

Sally Knights
James Renshaw

Great Clarendon Street, Oxford OX2 6DP

Oxford University Press is a department of the University of Oxford.

It furthers the University's objective of excellence in research, scholarship, and education by publishing worldwide in

Oxford New York
Auckland Cape Town Dar es Salaam Hong Kong Karachi
Kuala Lumpur Madrid Melbourne Mexico City Nairobi
New Delhi Shanghai Taipei Toronto

With offices in

Argentina Austria Brazil Chile Czech Republic France Greece Guatemala Hungary Italy Japan South Korea Poland Portugal Singapore Switzerland Thailand Turkey Ukraine Vietnam

Oxford is a registered trade mark of Oxford University Press
in the UK and in certain other countries

First published 2009

British Library Cataloguing in Publication Data

Data available

ISBN 978 019 832930 5

10 9 8 7 6 5 4 3 2 1

Printed in Great Britain by Bell & Bain, Glasgow

Paper used in the production of this book is a natural, recyclable product made from wood grown in sustainable forests. The manufacturing process conforms to the environmental regulations of the country of origin.

Acknowledgements

The authors and publisher would like to thank Paul Buckley for valuable comments on "Tackling the written examination", Kim Richardson (editor) and Carolyn Gibson (design manager). Page make-up is by Q2AMedia, New Delhi.

The Publisher is grateful to Penguin books for permission to reproduce brief extracts and quotations from the following publications: Homer, The Odyssey, trans E V Rieu, rev D C H Rieu, 1991 (2003 ed.); Ovid, Metamorphoses, trans. David Raeburn, 2004; Thucydides trans. Rex Warner (2008). Also to Bristol Classical Press for the extract on **p37** from Greek and Roman Education, Robin Barrow (1998) and Thames & Hudson for quotations on **pp 111, 132** from The Complete Pompeii, Joanne Berry (2007).

Every effort has been made to contact copyright holders of material reproduced in this book. If notified, the Publisher will be pleased to rectify any errors or omissions at the earliest opportunity.

Contents

Introduction 4

1 City Life in the Classical World (Unit A351) 6

Introduction 6

Athens 8

Rome 15

2 Epic and Myth (Unit A352) 21

Introduction 21

Homer, *The Odyssey* 22

Ovid, *Metamorphoses* 28

3 Community Life in the Classical World (Unit A353) 33

Introduction 33

Sparta 35

Pompeii 41

4 Tackling the written examination 48

5 Culture and Society in the Classical World: the Controlled Assessment (Unit A354) 53

Introduction 53

Sophocles, *Antigone* 57

Aristophanes, *Lysistrata* 59

The Olympic Games 61

Virgil, *The Aeneid* 63

Pliny, *Letters* 65

Roman Britain 67

Appendix 1 List of recordings 69

Appendix 2 Tyrtaios (Diehl³ 1.1.9) 71

Handouts 1–4 Sample essay responses 72

Introduction

The Teacher's Handbook runs parallel to the student Reader, adopting the same format of working in turn through each unit from the specification. It provides further factual information about the unit content, suggestions for resources for both student and teacher, ideas about how to teach the material and suggestions for student assignments.

Both the Reader and the Teacher's Handbook are underpinned by the aims of the course:

- to encourage students to be inspired and moved by the ancient world
- to actively engage students in the process of enquiry into the ancient world
- to help students to acquire knowledge and understanding through the study of primary source material
- to develop awareness of the continuing influence of the Romans and Greeks on later times, and to look at differences and similarities between them and us
- to encourage students to develop and apply analytical and evaluative skills, and make informed personal responses to the material studied.

Information about the scheme of assessment for each unit is provided at the front of the Reader; the precise content appears in the Teacher's Handbook at the head of the relevant section. The complete specification is available on the OCR website. Apart from the specification itself, it is important to look at the examination papers and mark schemes, sample schemes of work, the teacher guide to the controlled assessment and the annually updated resource lists.

Higher and foundation tier students are not addressed separately in the Reader, but the needs of both groups of students are borne in mind. The content and assessment objectives are the same for both tiers and the activities suggested are appropriate for both. The 'Taking it further' boxes in the Reader invite more independent exploration and so may be more appropriate for higher tier students. Decisions about the level of entry are generally made quite late on in the course, and exposing all students to the same information keeps their options open for longer. Detailed factual knowledge will form the core of their answers, be they multiple choice or essays.

The first decision to make is which options to teach. The answer, as for all things classical, lies in Delphi: *Know thyself* (and thy students). Choose the options for which you have the knowledge and resources, and which will at the same time appeal to your students. It is possible to choose all Greek options, for example, Athens, Sparta, Homer and (for the controlled assessment) Aristophanes, Sophocles or the Olympic Games. Likewise you can study just Roman topics, or have a more historical bias or a more literary one. There is an advantage in choosing from one of the examined units an option which will provide the underpinning knowledge for the controlled assessment, for example Rome for Pliny's *Letters* or the *Aeneid*, Athens for Aristophanes or Sophocles, particularly if you have to cover the course in a limited time. On the other hand, the study of unrelated topics can be rewarding in the breadth and variety it offers.

Chapter 4 below (Tackling the written examination) provides the answers to the questions discussed in the equivalent chapter of the Reader. It also includes two pairs of sample essays. The first of each pair is written by a competent student and gains high marks; the second scores lower marks because of a weakness in responding to one of the assessment criteria. Teachers might like to present students with similar sets of essays for their options, arm them with the assessment criteria and a red pen and let them do the marking. Finding weaknesses in the work of a third party always seems to be embraced so much more readily than self-criticism!

The Teacher's Handbook also gives suggestions about how to tackle the controlled assessment (see chapter 5 below). This new, and for some perhaps daunting, method of assessment becomes much less daunting if you approach it as an examination for which the student is given the question in advance and has to research the primary source material in order to answer it. The essay question will be one that can be answered at varying levels, thus accommodating students of different abilities.

The chapters on the various units give website addresses for specific research. The following addresses provide the teacher with some general classics sites which make excellent starting points. As a general rule, the internet is good for visual material, but it is difficult for GCSE students to assess the reliability of the text on many sites.

- **www.jact.org** JACT is the national association for Classics teachers.
- **www.arlt.co.uk** ARLT has among other things a calendar of all forthcoming Classics events such as TV programmes and theatre productions, a blog and a collection of resources for lending to members.
- **www.classicspage.com** The Classics Pages are full of stimulating activities which are bound to inspire students. There is an interactive Lysistrata game, the truth about the Cyclops (the dwarf elephant theory!), an Olympic Games quiz and links to lots of useful sites.
- **www.classics.ox.ac.uk/outreach/** Oxford Outreach provides support for the teacher.
- **www.perseus.tufts.edu** Perseus is a huge academic site excellent for research purposes – includes most ancient texts and many images.
- **www.vroma.org** is excellent for images of the Roman world.
- **www.insearchofthegreeks.com** This is a companion site to the book of the same name by James Renshaw. The parallel Roman version is due in 2011.
- **www.actorsofdionysus.com** Actors of Dionysus is a touring company specialising in Greek drama.
- **www.cambridgescp.com** The Cambridge Latin Course has excellent links for material about Pompeii and Roman life at the right level for your students.

1 City Life in the Classical World (Unit A351)

Introduction

Athens and Rome are the two iconic cities of the classical world. This unit of the GCSE course allows students to explore various central elements of one of these societies; as a result, they should be able to develop an understanding of what life was like for a range of different groups in either city – men and women, boys and girls, citizen and non-citizen, slave and free. As the OCR specification makes clear, it is important that students learn to draw comparisons between their own society and the ancient society which they are studying.

Clearly the first thing a teacher needs to decide is which of the two options to teach. This is a no-lose situation: both options promise interest, variety and good resources. One of the great advantages of teaching Classical Civilisation is that the material is never dull! However, it is worth looking at how each option is distinctive, and what considerations you might factor into your decision.

There are some areas of great similarity between the Rome and Athens options. The topic areas headed 'The gods' ('State gods and goddesses' in the Rome option), 'Temples' and 'Sacrifice' are very similar in both since the Romans effectively adopted these aspects of Greek religion. In addition, the Athens topic areas 'The oikos' and 'Education' have many overlaps with the Rome topic areas 'Life in the home' and 'Education' since Greek culture influenced the Romans in these areas too.

The most distinctive topics in the Athens option are 'The Panathenaia', 'The City Dionysia' and 'Tragedy and comedy':

- The **Panathenaia** topic really builds on the religion topics of the gods, temples and sacrifice; it focuses on the festival to celebrate the birthday of Athena, the patron goddess of the city. During this festival there were a variety of athletic, musical and cultural events, including the presentation of a new peplos (body-length garment) to a statue of Athena on the Acropolis. It gives the student the opportunity to examine Athens on its 'national day', and what the events might tell us about the city and how its people saw themselves.
- The **City Dionysia** topic similarly focuses on an important religious festival, at which playwrights presented plays in a competition in the city's grand theatre. It focuses on how the Athenians prepared for the festival, the other events which surrounded the presentation of the plays, and how the Athenians watched and judged their plays. As a festival, it could perhaps be compared to a film festival today, and this will be a comparison students might enjoy making.
- The **Tragedy and comedy** topic builds on the previous one by examining the two types of play that were put on at the festival. This allows students to explore many elements of the plays, including theatre design, actors and costumes, and is well suited to students who have an interest in the theatre.

The most distinctive topics in the Rome option are 'A typical day at the Colosseum' and 'A typical day at the races'. It would be fair to say that these are far more 'bloodthirsty' topics than anything offered in the Athens option.

- **A typical day at the Colosseum** examines a topic area with which most students are likely to have some familiarity already, perhaps by watching documentaries or the film *Gladiator*. However, it is more than just studying types of gladiators, as other activities of the amphitheatre, such as executions and slaughters of animals, also feature. Another important element is the way in which such shows were heavily political and of great propaganda value for emperors. In short: horrifying brutality, excitement and politics!

- **A typical day at the races** looks at the chariot racing held at the Circus Maximus in Rome. Again, there is the bloody prospect of crashes and injuries here, but the emphasis is really on the skill of the charioteers, the spectacle of the day and the excitement and behaviour of the crowd. There is plenty of scope for comparison with modern sporting events.

Another factor which may influence your choice could be the choices you make in other teaching units. For example, if you have decided to study Homer's *Odyssey* in the Epic and Myth unit, then you may feel that you wish to study Athens to allow your students to develop an understanding of the Greek gods whom they will meet in this text; for the same reason, you may feel that the Rome option might tie in better with Ovid's *Metamorphoses*.

Some teachers may decide that they wish to keep their options 'all Greek' (Athens, Homer's *Odyssey* and Sparta) or 'all Roman' (Rome, Pompeii, Ovid's *Metamorphoses*). While such combinations do link into each other more closely in some ways, it is also true that students are likely to enjoy some exposure to both the Greeks and the Romans; and it is important not to forget that there are very many overlaps between the two civilisations (for example, Ovid's *Metamorphoses* are primarily based on tales from Greek mythology).

Both options are well resourced by books and the internet, and teachers should have no problem finding additional material for the course. It is probably fair to say that the Rome option has some excellent audio-visual facilities in the areas of gladiators and chariot-racing. On the other hand, if you are teaching about Athenian drama, there may well be a current production of a Greek tragedy or comedy which you could take your students to see.

Athens

The focus of this option is the everyday life of an ancient Greek citizen in one of the most flourishing city states in ancient times. Candidates should have a basic understanding of the concept of democracy as practised by Athens.

Candidates are required to have knowledge and understanding of the following main areas of Athenian life:

- religion – its role and importance in the lives of the Greeks, including a number of festivals;
- the family in Athens – the roles and duties of its individual members and their homes;
- entertainment in Athens – the symbolism and appeal of these activities in the context of Athenian society.

Candidates will be expected to respond to literary and visual sources and to draw conclusions about the values and priorities of the citizens of Athens and the image Athens portrayed to other city states in Greece.

Specific topics:

The gods	Zeus, Hera, Demeter, Poseidon, Hephaistos, Apollo, Artemis, Athene, Aphrodite, Ares, Dionysos (and his companion maenads and satyrs), Hermes. Their responsibilities and how they are typically represented in Greek art.
Temples	Religious functions: the position of the altar, the cult statue, use by worshippers.
Sacrifice	Its purpose, surroundings, officials, animals, the ritual and its significance.
The Panathenaia	The programme, the participants, its importance to the Athenians, the religious and political content; the Parthenon frieze showing the Panathenaia.
The City Dionysia	Participants, programme, judging. The religious, political and theatrical content.
Tragedy and comedy	Actors: typical roles, masks, costumes and acting styles of tragic and comic actors and chorus members. The theatre: the shape, layout, position and use in performance of the *skene*, *proskene*, orchestra, altar, *parodoi*, the *mekhane*, the *ekkuklema*, scenery, and sound effects. The Theatre of Dionysos as a typical example.
The *oikos*	The husband: his duties and role as *kyrios*, property rights, legal rights. The wife: her status as *kyria*, duties within the household, property rights. *Symposia*: organisation, guests, entertainment, purposes. An Athenian house: the basic design (courtyard, *andron and gynaikon*), layout, furniture, and the appearance of the rooms and areas. Slaves: skilled and unskilled, ways to become a slave, the purchasing of slaves, duties inside and outside the home for both male and female slaves, opportunities for freedom.
Education	The education of boys and girls in preparation for their adult roles. The *paidotribes*, the *grammatistes*, the *kitharistes*, the *paidagogos*, the *palaistra*.

Key resources

When teaching Athens, there are some key resources which should help any teacher. The first half of Peter Connolly's book *The Ancient City* (OUP) is informative and has numerous fine drawings and illustrations reconstructing life in the city. *In Search of the Greeks* (Bristol Classical Press) by James Renshaw is purpose written for Classical Civilisation students and gives a more detailed focus on the city of Athens. Further reading for a teacher is also provided by *The World of Athens* (JACT).

This topic is also well served by the internet. **www.insearchofthegreeks.com** is a website designed to back up the book, and contains many photos of classical sites. **www.ancientgreece.co.uk** is a website designed by the British Museum, and contains many interactive resources for students to work through. **http://www.bbc.co.uk/history/ancient/greeks/** is the BBC's site on ancient Greece and has some good information on Athenian democracy.

The context: Athens, Greece and democracy

The first point to be made is that the region of Greece did not become a single country until the late 4th century BC, later than the high point of Athenian society in the 5th century, which is the focus of this unit. Until the late 4th century, Greece was a region of many different independent cities, known as city-states. The inhabitants of all these cities spoke the same language, worshipped the same gods and enjoyed a common literature, but that is not to say that they all got along well. In fact, they were often at war with one another.

Originally, the Greek cities were to be found in mainland Greece – places like Athens, Sparta, Corinth, Thebes and Megara. However, from the 8th century BC a growth in the population led Greeks to emigrate and live further afield; initially, new cities were established around the Aegean Sea, either on the islands or on its northern and eastern seaboards; however, the region soon expanded to include the shores of the Black Sea, north Africa and, in particular, southern Italy and Sicily.

By the 5th century, Athens and Sparta were the two most powerful city-states in the Greek world. After they combined with others to see off the Persian invasions of 490–479, a cold war broke out between the two cities. Athens joined with many other cities to come up with a common defensive alliance to maintain a fleet to protect them against further Persian attacks. As Athens was the largest city and had the largest fleet, it effectively took charge of the navy, and the other cities had to provide Athens with either ships or money by way of a contribution.

After peace had been made with the Persians in the 450s, some cities in the alliance wanted to stop paying for the joint defence force. However, Athens wouldn't let them and threatened force. It was at this moment that the 'alliance' effectively became an Athenian Empire, with all the other cities being forced to continue paying Athens tribute. The Athenian leader at this stage, Pericles, instituted a massive building programme to rebuild the city which had been left in ruins by the invading Persians in 480. During the 440s–430s, the great buildings of Athens, including the Parthenon on the Acropolis, were designed and completed. It is against the backdrop of these times that the Panathenaia and the City Dionysia, both included on our specification, were held.

The later 5th century was a period of growing tragedy for Athens. It spent many of the years between 431 and 404 at war with Sparta, which finally ended in defeat. Athens lost her empire, although she ultimately managed to preserve her democratic system. The city lived on relatively successfully through the 4th century until Philip of Macedon (to the north of Greece) invaded and unified the whole of Greece under his rule by 338. Athens' glory days were behind her.

The specification requires that 'candidates should have a basic understanding of democracy as practised by Athens', and there is a section about this in the Reader (pages 25–26). For a detailed exploration of this topic, see chapter 5 of *In Search of the Greeks* by James Renshaw (Bristol Classical Press), or *Athenian Democracy* by John Thorley (Routledge).

There are a few important points which could be made here about the Athenian democratic system. The first was that the only citizens in the city were Athenian males – women, foreigners and slaves were all prevented from voting. It has been estimated that the population of Athens in the 5th century might have been 300,000, of which about a third were slaves. Based on this population estimate, it is likely that the actual citizen population was between only 30,000 and 50,000.

However, there is no doubt that all citizens got involved with running their city. The assembly, where laws were made, met four times a month and any citizen could attend (thus the Athenians did not have 'representative' democracy as we do today – any citizen could vote on any issue). As we can see from our specification, the democratic system spilled over into every area of life – both the Panathenaia and the City Dionysia incorporate democratic elements into their events.

Finally, it is worth mentioning that the Athenians felt inordinately proud of their democratic system. It is something which they had come up with themselves and which defined them as a people.

Although students do not need to know the information contained above, it makes some sense to start the option by giving them some sense of the history and geography of the city in relation to the rest of Greece.

Teaching suggestions

- For a general historical outline, you could hand out a timeline based on the information above (although remember that students do not need to learn these dates).
- It is also important to hand out a map of the Greek world so that students can locate Athens. It may be worth finding a map which includes the Aegean Sea and west coast of modern Turkey, as the whole of this area was entirely Greek at this stage.
- It will be worthwhile for your students to have a map of the city of Athens. This way, they can identify places such as the Theatre of Dionysos, the Acropolis, the agora and the Panathenaic Way, all of which feature in the two festivals covered in the specification. A very good map can be found online at **http://plato-dialogues.org/tools/athensim.htm**

The gods (Reader, pages 17–20)

The Greek gods had been worshipped for many centuries by the time that we are focusing on; there is written evidence of their worship in the middle of the 2nd millennium BC. The Greeks believed that the Olympian gods were the third generation in their family. First had come Gaia (Earth) who had coupled with Ouranos (Sky) and they had had various children, including Rhea, Cronos and the Giants. Urged on by his angry mother, Cronos overthrew his father Ouranos, castrating him in the process (his sperm fell into the sea of Cyprus and produced the goddess Aphrodite).

Cronos and Rhea then married and themselves produced six children: Hestia, Demeter, Hera, Hades, Poseidon and Zeus. Cronos received a prophecy that his son would grow up to overthrow him, and so he swallowed each child as they were born. However, when the youngest, Zeus, was born, Rhea tricked Cronos into swallowing a rock instead. Zeus was smuggled away and grew up elsewhere. When he reached adulthood, he overthrew both Cronos and his whole generation, forcing him to vomit up his siblings. Zeus became king of the new group of gods who made their home on Mt Olympus; they therefore became known as the Olympians.

Greeks believed that the victory of the Olympian gods over earlier generations of gods symbolised the victory of order over chaos. This idea comes into our specification with the peplos for Athena made each year at the Panathenaia, which always displayed the victory of the Olympians over the giants.

The British Museum has an excellent site which focuses on the twelve Olympians: **http://www.ancientgreece.co.uk/gods/explore/exp_set.html**

The Greek gods were at the centre of many of the stories of Greek mythology, and this is a rich source of material for teachers. It would be worth exploring one story (or more) about each god to give students a flavour of that god's personality. Here are some suggestions, although they are certainly not exhaustive. All of them can be found widely in mythology books or on the internet.

Zeus: If you are studying Homer's *Odyssey*, you might want to tie in your teaching with Zeus' role as the protector of strangers and travellers in the poem. In particular, Odysseus' claim to be under the protection of Zeus while visiting the Cyclops in Book 9 is worth looking at. Alternatively, the episode in Homer's *Iliad* (22.209–213) when Zeus weighs up the lives of Achilles and Hector in his golden scales is very dramatic, and shows him as a god who upholds fate. If you are studying Ovid's *Metamorphoses*, then Jupiter's handling of the assembly in Book 1 shows him in regal mode.

Poseidon: Again, students of Homer's *Odyssey* will want to examine this text for evidence of the god of the sea's personality. In particular, his pursuit of Odysseus in a storm at 5.282–381 is worth reading. Away from this text, the story of how Poseidon competed with Athena to become the patron god of Athens is also relevant to our specification.

Hera: Since Hera was most often seen in a rage at her husband's infidelities, it would be worth at looking at a couple of such stories. By examining her jealousies of Leto (mother of Apollo and Artemis) and Semele (mother of Dionysos), your students will also learn about how three other Olympian gods came to be born. If you are studying Ovid's *Metamorphoses* then the stories of Juno's (Hera's) jealousy of Io, Europa and Semele tie in well with a study of this goddess.

Demeter: The story of the abduction of her daughter Persephone by Hades is a very beautiful myth and a superb example of how the Greeks used their gods to explain natural phenomena which they couldn't otherwise understand. It can be read (with Roman names) in Ovid's *Metamorphoses*, 5.341–661.

Ares, Aphrodite and **Hephaistos:** These three can be covered in one famous story from the *Odyssey* (8.266–366), in which the lovers Ares and Aphrodite are trapped in bed by Aphrodite's husband Hephaistos. Much comedy value to be had here!

Athene: There are two important stories to cover here – her birth from the head of Zeus, and how she competed with Poseidon to become the patron goddess of Athens.

Apollo and **Artemis:** You may already have read of how they came to be born on the island of Delos. You may also wish to read about how Apollo became infatuated by a nymph called Daphne (leading to the laurel becoming his sacred tree), while the story of Artemis and Actaeon is a classic.

Dionysos: Students may already have read of his mother Semele's affair with Zeus and the nature of his birth; in addition, the story of his return to Thebes and punishment of Pentheus (and other Thebans) gives a good profile of the god and also includes important details about the Maenads.

Hermes: The first day of his life, when he stole Apollo's cattle and invented the lyre, was eventful and tells us a lot about him. Students of Homer's *Odyssey* will be interested that he helps Odysseus in Book 10 by giving him the plant *moly*.

There are other ways in which you can encourage your students to develop their knowledge of the gods. Here are some suggestions.

Teaching suggestions

- They could research and draw up a family tree of the Olympian gods.
- They could be presented with images of the gods from Greek art and asked to identify them. This is particularly useful for developing students' ability to respond

to visual sources. You can find an excellent series of images at **http://www.theoi.com/GalleryK1.html**

- If you want to give things a 'modern' spin, then you could suggest to students that they imagine that the gods had profiles on social networking sites such as Facebook. What would Zeus' home page look like? What would he give under 'personal information'? What would he say under 'relationship status'?
- You could ask students to draw their own work of art incorporating one or more of the gods and illustrating some of their qualities.

This topic also offers rich areas for comparisons with modern religious beliefs. As a polytheistic system, there are some clear parallels with Hinduism (with which Greek religion almost certainly shares some ancestry); one source of discussion might be about the different natures of polytheistic and monotheistic belief systems.

There is also a lot to be made of the relationship between religion and morality. The Olympians did not set out to set a moral example to humans; in fact, they behaved appallingly at times. This is often very different from modern notions of a God who is perfectly good (although it could be argued, for example, that the God of the Old Testament is at times harsh and vindictive).

Temples and sacrifice

(Reader, pages 20–22)

These two topics have been joined together in this section as they complement one another closely. They are both slightly more 'functional' topics following the rich variety offered by the Olympian gods, but sacrifice in particular is an important element in the Panathenaia and City Dionysia topics which follow and so students need a sound knowledge of it.

Temples started to appear in the Greek world from the 8th century BC; in these early days, they were probably influenced by the much older temples of Egypt. From the beginning, they played an important role in the developing Greek societies. Greeks generally did not build grand private buildings; it was to their public temples that they looked for architectural inspiration. Sanctuaries were the focus of worship for a particular god (or group of gods), and temples were built to glorify those gods. Another point to be made about temples is that they often fitted very well into their natural surroundings, either by standing out on a high point (such as the temples of the Acropolis, or the Hephaistion, a temple built on a small hill by the Athenian agora), or by fitting well in a place of natural beauty (such as Bassae in the Peloponnese).

Sacrifice is common to all ancient cultures. It is really a practice which survives from much earlier human times, when people were hunter-gatherers. Hunting one's prey was a daily challenge and, when successful, men wanted to thank the gods for their help in their success (*A Short History of Myth* by Karen Armstrong (Canongate) has an excellent short explanation of this).

It is almost impossible to imagine Greek society without sacrifice – it really was a daily process. People would sacrifice to the gods to ask help or give thanks for all sorts of reasons; for example, when preparing to go to war, marry, sow, harvest, travel, not to mention at any festival. It is also important to be aware of the social importance of sacrifice; most sacrifices took place in public, people wore their best clothes and their piety was very much on display. In addition, there was an important communal element: people came together to share in the process, and this culminated in the meal afterwards – meat was rarely eaten by Greeks except after a sacrifice.

Teaching suggestions

- A fruitful way to examine Greek temples is to compare them with modern places of worship, thinking in particular about some of the key differences: the fact that worship took place outside the building (where the altar was found); the fact that the temple was believed to be the *home* of a god, symbolised by the cult statue; the fact that different gods were worshipped at different temples. In addition, it is worth examining the architectural significance of ancient and modern religious buildings.

- Although not required on the specification, teachers may want to give stronger candidates some extension by looking at some basic temple architecture. You might look at the orders of architecture (Doric, Ionic and Corinthian), as well as the sculptural importance of the pediments, frieze and metopes. This British Museum site allows visitors to 'build their own Greek temple': **http://www.ancientgreece.co.uk/acropolis/challenge/cha_set.html**
- Specific temples to examine in Athens: the Hephaistion by the agora is an excellent example of a traditionally designed temple; the Parthenon, Erechtheion and Temple of Athena Nike on the Acropolis are all fascinating but not perfect examples of a typical Greek temple.
- For teaching sacrifice, it is worth looking at a very good example of a sacrifice from the *Odyssey* (3.430–463). Ask your students to list all the elements which match up to the description of a sacrifice in the Reader, and then to see if anything has been left out (no two sacrifices were exactly the same!).
- There is also plenty of scope here for comparison with the modern world. Today, we eat more meat than the Greeks ever did but, unlike them, most of us never see the animals killed. Students might compare a Greek sacrifice with a modern abattoir, and think about which gives the animal more dignity. There is the opportunity for discussion about the ethics of eating meat and treatment of animals.

The Panathenaia (Reader, pages 23–25)

It is probably best for a teacher to do some separate reading for background information on this topic. Both Peter Connolly's *The Ancient City* (OUP, pages 80–87) and *In Search of the Greeks* by James Renshaw (pages 29–35) have detailed descriptions of the various activities. The association of the Parthenon frieze with the Panathenaic procession is controversial, although it is the most commonly held theory. A good analysis of the issues can be found at **http://en.wikipedia.org/wiki/Parthenon_Frieze#Interpretation**

Teaching suggestions

The Panathenaia can be approached by encouraging students to:

- Explore the sporting events held at the festival. One way to do this is by examining images of Panathenaic amphorae – a Google image search of this topic will provide a multitude of options. Alternatively, both books mentioned above have some good information about the sporting events.
- Research the myth of the battle between the Olympians and the giants, which was depicted on Athene's peplos. The more creative students may enjoy coming up with their own artistic representation of the peplos.
- Find out about the two musical instruments used in the musical competitions. The following site is excellent: **http://www.oeaw.ac.at/kal/agm/**
- Create their own account of the Panathenaic procession; this will allow them to imagine how the sights and sounds of the event might have been experienced.
- Learn about the Parthenon frieze (although this is probably for brighter students as detailed knowledge is not required by the specification). The following British Museum website is very informative: **http://www.ancientgreece.co.uk/acropolis/story/sto_set.html**
- Compare the Panathenaia with similar events in the modern world: students may like to look at a religious festival (e.g. Christmas, Eid, Diwali) or an important national civic festival (e.g. St Patrick's Day for Irish people).

The sporting and cultural events also invite comparison with modern equivalents such as the Olympics or a music festival (e.g. Glastonbury).

The City Dionysia, tragedy and comedy

(Reader, pages 26–31)

These two topics have been joined together in this section as they are so interlinked. As with the Panathenaia, it is advisable for a teacher to do some further reading for background information: Chapter 3 of *In Search of the Greeks* by James Renshaw has a thorough outline of Athenian drama.

Teaching suggestions

As with the Panathenaia, there are a variety of approaches you could take:

- It is worth comparing the City Dionysia with a modern arts festival, for example, the Cannes Film Festival or the Edinburgh festival. When looking at the judging process, there is a natural comparison to be made with modern 'voting' TV shows such as *Strictly Come Dancing* or the *X Factor*.
- Students could try to draw up a table of similarities and differences between acting in a modern play and an ancient tragedy or comedy, as well as examine the similarities and differences between an ancient and a modern theatre building.
- More creative students might want to draw or design their own theatre masks, while others might be encouraged to give a written account of watching a play.

The oikos and education

(Reader, pages 12–17)

These two topics have been joined together in this section as they overlap closely. For background reading, Peter Connolly's *The Ancient City* (Part I, chapters 4–6) has some excellent material and images, while chapter 4 of *In Search of the Greeks* by James Renshaw has covers the specification material in more detail.

Teaching suggestions

- The most obvious comparison to make is with the students' own home life. There is plenty of scope for discussion here about the changed roles of men and women at home (although the 'Athenian' model was in place in this country until relatively recently and remains so in other parts of the world). Likewise, a student may enjoy trying to compare his or her home with those of Athens. The British Museum has an excellent site on Greek houses: **http://www.ancientgreece.co.uk/dailylife/challenge/cha_set.html**
- When discussing slavery, it is worth having an overview of the history of slavery and the fact that it has only really been abolished relatively recently. Moreover, there remain many people who are effectively or literally enslaved today – the website **www.antislavery.org** has some excellent information about this. Ask you students to come up with a definition of 'slavery'.
- Students may also want to reflect on whether slaves automatically had bad lives. If a slave lived with a compassionate and fair master, was his life actually better than a poor Athenian who struggled to provide for his family?
- When examining education, there is clearly scope for some fun in comparing Athenian education with their own. Students may enjoy writing about 'a day in the life of an Athenian student', or coming up with an end of term report for an Athenian boy (although no such thing really existed).
- The education topic is also an opportunity to reflect on education as a universal right. The fact that neither girls nor the poorest boys were educated was by no means unique to Athenian society, and indeed that pattern still continues in parts of the world today.

Rome

The focus of this option is the everyday life of an ancient Roman citizen in the capital of the empire. Candidates should have a basic understanding of Rome's status as the ruler of a vast empire.

Candidates are required to have knowledge and understanding of three main areas of Roman life:

- religion – its role and importance in the lives of the Romans;
- the family in Rome – the roles and duties of its individual members;
- entertainment and recreation in Rome – the appeal of these leisure activities in the context of Roman society and their value to the emperor in the control of its people.

Candidates will be expected to respond to sources and to draw conclusions about the values and priorities of the citizens of Rome and the image Rome portrayed to the rest of her empire.

Specific topics:

State gods and goddesses	Jupiter, Neptune, Mercury, Mars, Pluto (Hades), Apollo, Juno, Venus, Minerva, Diana, Vesta and Ceres. Their responsibilities and symbols and how they are typically represented in Roman art.
Temples	Religious and other functions: the position of the altar, the cult statue, use by worshippers.
Sacrifice	Its purpose, surroundings, officials, animals, the ritual from the selection of the animal to the disposal of the remains.
Life in the home	The role of the *paterfamilias:* his rights over family members and slaves, his involvement in the education of his son, duties connected with religion, family finance; his responsibilities towards his clients. The wife: status, rights and duties, daily activities, spinning and weaving, the supervision of slaves, the wife as mother. The dinner party (*cena*): the organisation, guests, entertainment, purposes. Slaves: ways to become a slave, skilled and unskilled slaves, the purchasing of slaves, duties inside and outside the home for both male and female slaves, opportunities for freedom.
Education	The education of boys and girls in preparation for their adult roles. Subjects studied at the schools of the *litterarius, grammaticus* and *rhetor;* school equipment (*stilus*, wax tablet, pen, ink, papyrus).
A typical day at the Colosseum	The Colosseum: the arena, size, access, seating, structure. Animal shows: types of animal, the *bestiarius*, men versus animals, performing animals, fights between animals, hunts. Executions. Gladiator shows: origins as funerary honours, types of gladiator*; retiarius, secutors (samnite, myrmillo)*, armour, weaponry, typical training for fights (*ludi gladiatorii*), oaths, status. Audience involvement. The significance of the shows for both the Emperor and his citizens.
A typical day at the races	The *Circus Maximus:* the day's events. The arena, its structure, size, the seating, the track, the *spina*, the *metae*, the *carceres*. The teams and colours, the dangers, the status of charioteers and horses, public attitudes, audience involvement, betting, the social significance of such events.

Key resources

When teaching Rome, there are some key resources which should help any teacher. The second half of Peter Connolly's book *The Ancient City* (OUP) is informative and has numerous fine drawings and illustrations reconstructing life in the city. *In Search of the Romans* (Bristol Classical Press) by James Renshaw is due out in 2011; it will give classical students a more detailed focus on the topics in this syllabus. For a teacher, *The World of Rome* (JACT) is a fount of knowledge, while *Daily Life in Ancient Rome* (Penguin) by Jerome Carcopino is also very good, and gives detailed information about the ancient written sources.

On the internet, **http://www.bbc.co.uk/history/ancient/romans/** is the excellent BBC site on the Romans, with plenty of information and images. **http://www.omnibusol.com/anrome.html** contains numerous links to sites on the Roman world, many of which are very good. The website of the Cambridge Latin Course, **http://www.cambridgescp.com/page.php?p=clc^top^home**, also contains many links to the Roman world for each of its chapters.

The context: the Roman Empire

As the saying goes, Rome was not built in a day. The foundation of the city seems to be dated to the 8th century BC, although for many centuries it was a small settlement in central Italy and not even the most powerful city in the region. Perhaps the first definitive moment in its history came in 509 BC, when it overthrew its traditional kings and set up a new and more radical system of government – the republic. This involved the election of various magistrates to positions of political importance each year. The two most important magistrates were known as the consuls. They held the most political power, but no law could be passed without them both agreeing to it; this way, no single individual could gain too much power, as had happened under the kings. The magistrates were advised by the Senate, a body consisting of a group of elders (senators) from aristocratic clans.

Slowly the city started to expand its territorial control; in the 4th century it started to advance into other parts of Italy, but the key moment in its history came in the 3rd century during the wars with Carthage in North Africa. Since Carthage controlled much of the western Mediterranean, it was really a battle for control of the seas. When the Romans finally won, they became powerful throughout lands as far afield as Spain, France and North Africa. Rome had started to build an empire. This process continued in the 2nd century with their advance into the eastern Mediterranean. When they conquered Greece in 146 BC they became the masters of the old Greek empire, which spread through places as far afield as modern Turkey, Syria, the middle east, Egypt and Libya. Rome truly was now the master of the world.

The 1st century BC was a turbulent one in the Roman world. The political system of the republic, which had been set up when the city was small, was not a suitable or effective way to run a large empire. Rome descended into a series of civil wars, at the heart of which were a series of generals, the musclemen of the day. Julius Caesar was one of these; his campaigns had seen the conquest of the whole of modern France and Belgium. However, when he returned to Rome and set himself up as the sole dictator, other senators successfully plotted his assassination. After a further series of civil wars, Julius Caesar's heir Augustus emerged as the victor and established himself as the first Roman emperor. Although the republican system of magistrates and senate remained in place, in effect it was the emperor who had the final say in political matters.

This was the arrangement which stayed in place for the next four centuries as Rome ruled the known world. It was only in the early 5th century AD that the barbarians living on the borders of the empire started to overrun Roman towns; the Romans had become too easy in their wealth and power and were unused to defending their borders. The empire collapsed and Rome was sacked in 410, never to return to her former glory.

Although students do not need to know the information contained above, it makes some sense to start the option by giving them some sense of the history and geography of Rome and its empire.

Teaching suggestions

- For a general historical outline, you could hand out a timeline based on the information above (although remember that students do not need to learn these dates).
- It is also important to hand out a map of the Roman Empire so that students can locate Rome and understand the extend of its power.
- It will be worthwhile for your students to have a map of the city of Rome. This way, they can identify places such as the Forum, the Colosseum and the Circus Maximus.

State gods and goddesses

(Reader, pages 38–41)

The Romans generally adopted the Greek Olympian gods as their own, simply changing their names (apart from Apollo, who kept his Greek name). There were a few local stories added to the traditional mythologies of these gods, but by and large their characters remained much the same. Therefore, when teaching this topic, a teacher would greatly benefit from reading through the material about the Greek gods in the Athens option (see pages 17–20).

The British Museum has an excellent site which focuses on the twelve Olympians (although they only have their Greek names on this site): **http://www.ancientgreece.co.uk/gods/explore/exp_set.html**

Students of Ovid's *Metamorphoses* will know that the Romans loved the myths associated with the Olympian gods every bit as much as the Greeks did. It would be worth exploring one story (or more) about each god to give students a flavour of that god's personality. Here are some suggestions, although they are certainly not exhaustive. All of them can be found widely in mythology books or on the internet. Many of the stories listed below are also listed under the Greek gods section of the Athens option.

Jupiter: If you are studying Homer's *Odyssey*, you might want to tie in your teaching with Zeus' role as the protector of strangers and travellers in the poem. In particular, Odysseus' claim to be under the protection of Zeus while visiting the Cyclops in Book 9 is worth looking at. Alternatively, those who are studying Ovid's *Metamorphoses* might wish to look closely at how he presides over the assembly as king of the gods in Book 1. His relationship with his wife is also shown up in the set text for the specification by his affairs with Semele, Io and Europa.

Juno: Again, the prescribed books of Ovid's *Metamorphoses* show Juno at her jealous best in her treatment of Semele, Io and Europa and Echo.

Neptune: Again, students of Homer's *Odyssey* will want to examine this text for evidence of Poseidon's personality. In particular, his pursuit of Odysseus in a storm at 5.282–381 is worth reading. From Ovid's *Metamorphoses*, the story of how he protects Mestra puts him in a good light.

Ceres and **Pluto**: The story of the abduction of Ceres' daughter Proserpina by Pluto is a very beautiful myth and a superb example of how the Greeks and Romans used their gods to explain natural phenomena which they couldn't otherwise understand. The story can be read in Ovid's *Metamorphoses*, 5.341–661. From the sections of Ovid in the specification, Ceres' punishment of Erysichthon in Book 8 indicates her care for the natural world. Note that Pluto is not technically termed an 'Olympian' god as he lived below the earth rather than on Mt Olympus. However, he is the brother of both Jupiter and Neptune.

Mars, **Venus** (and **Vulcan**, although he is not included on the specification): These gods can be covered in one famous story from the *Odyssey* (8.266–366), in which the lovers Ares and Aphrodite are trapped in bed by Aphrodite's husband Hephaistos. Much comedy value to be had here! In addition, it is helpful to be aware of the importance of Mars and Venus to the city of Rome: Venus as the mother of Aeneas, who led the Trojans to Italy, while, some generations later, Aeneas' descendent Rhea Silva was impregnated by Mars to give birth to Romulus, the traditional founder of Rome, and his twin brother Remus.

Minerva: Students will enjoy the story of her birth from the head of Jupiter, while they may also like to read about her punishment of Arachne, which emphasises the goddess's responsibility of arts and crafts.

Apollo: The story of his love for Daphne in Book 1 of Ovid's *Metamorphoses* is highly entertaining. Students may also be interested to research his role as god of prophecy (at Delphi) and of sporting and musical contests.

Mercury: The first day of his life, when he stole Apollo's cattle and invented the lyre, was eventful and tells us a lot about him. Students of Homer's *Odyssey* will be interested that he helps Odysseus in Book 10 by giving him the plant *moly*.

Vesta: There are few myths about her, but it is well worth your students finding out about the temple of Vesta and the cult of the Vestal Virgins in Rome, as this was central to Roman state religion.

Teaching suggestions

- Students could research and draw up a family tree of the Olympian gods.
- They could be presented with images of the gods from Greek art (which was widely available in the Roman world) and asked to identify them. This is particularly useful for developing students' ability to respond to visual sources. You can find an excellent series of images at: **http://www.theoi.com/GalleryK1.html**
- If you want to give things a 'modern' spin, then you could suggest to students that they imagine that the gods had profiles on social networking sites such as Facebook. What would Jupiter's home page look like? What would he give under 'personal information'? What would he say under 'relationship status'?
- You could ask students to draw their own work of art incorporating one or more of the gods and illustrating some of their qualities.
- The Roman gods have given their names to many of the planets of the solar system and other stars. For extension, students could examine how each planet came to be named and why that particular god was chosen.
- Students may enjoy listening to excerpts from Gustav Holst's *The Planets Suite* and considering how each god's character is reflected in the music.

This topic also offers rich areas for comparisons with modern religious beliefs. As a polytheistic system, there are some clear parallels with Hinduism (with which Roman religion almost certainly shares some ancestry); one source of discussion might be about the different natures of polytheistic and monotheistic belief systems.

There is also a lot to be made of the relationship between religion and morality. The Olympians did not set out to set a moral example to humans; in fact, they behaved appallingly at times. This is often very different from modern notions of a God who is perfectly good (although it could be argued, for example, that the God of the Old Testament is at times harsh and vindictive).

Finally, students may enjoy finding out how the following English words are derived from the Roman gods: *jovial, mercurial, venereal, venerate, martial, cereal, June.*

Temples and sacrifice

(Reader, pages 41–42)

Both Roman temples and Roman sacrifices were influenced directly by the Greek world, and so it is worth reading the introduction to the equivalent topic in the Athens option for some background information here (see pages 20–22).

Teaching suggestions

- A fruitful way to examine Roman temples is to compare them with modern places of worship, thinking in particular about some of the key differences: the fact that worship took place outside the building (where the altar was found); the fact that the temple was believed to be the *home* of a god, symbolised by the cult statue; the fact that different gods were worshipped at different temples. In addition, it is worth examining the architectural significance of ancient and modern religious buildings.
- Although not required on the specification, teachers may want to give stronger candidates some extension by looking at some basic temple architecture (which the Romans inherited from the Greeks). You might look at the orders of architecture (Doric, Ionic and Corinthian), as well as the sculptural importance of the pediments, frieze and metopes. This British Museum site allows visitors to 'build their own Greek temple': **http://www.ancientgreece.co.uk/acropolis/challenge/cha_set.html**
- Specific temples to examine in Rome: the Temple of Saturn, the Temple of Capitoline Jupiter and, for something inspiring but unconventional, the Pantheon.
- For teaching sacrifice, the best literary example comes from a Greek text: Homer's *Odyssey* 3.430–463. Ask your students to list all the elements which match up to the description of a sacrifice in the Reader, and then to see if anything has been left out (no two sacrifices were exactly the same!). If you are keen to explore a Latin text, Ovid has an interesting 'animal's eye view' at *Metamorphoses* 15.60ff.
- There is also plenty of scope here for comparison with the modern world. Today, we never watch the deaths of the animals we eat. Students might compare a Roman sacrifice with a modern abattoir, and think about which gives the animal more dignity. There is the opportunity for discussion about the ethics of eating meat and treatment of animals.

Life in the home and education

(Reader, pages 32–38)

These two topics have been joined together in this section as they overlap closely. For background reading, Peter Connolly's *The Ancient City* (Part II, chapters 5–6) has some excellent material and images.

Teaching suggestions

- The most obvious comparison to make is with the students' own home life. There is plenty of scope for discussion here about the changed roles of men and women at home (although the 'Roman' model was in place in this country until relatively recently and remains so in other parts of the world). Likewise, a student may enjoy trying to compare his or her home with those of Rome.
- When discussing slavery, it is worth having an overview of the history of slavery and the fact that it has only really been abolished relatively recently. Moreover, there remain many people who are effectively or literally enslaved today – the website **www.antislavery.org** has some excellent information about this. Ask you students to come up with a definition of 'slavery'.
- Students may also want to reflect on whether slaves automatically had bad lives. If a slave lived with a compassionate and fair master, was his life actually better than a poor Roman who struggled to provide for his family?
- When examining education, there is clearly scope for some fun in comparing Roman education with their own. Students may enjoy writing about 'a day in the life of an Roman student', or coming up with an end of term report for an Roman boy (although no such thing really existed).

- The education topic is also an opportunity to reflect on education as a universal right. The fact that neither girls nor the poorest boys were educated was by no means unique to Roman society, and indeed that pattern still continues in parts of the world today.

A typical day at the Colosseum

(Reader, pages 43–47)

This is of course an ever popular topic with students. For some background reading, chapter 11 of Part II of Peter Connolly's *The Ancient City* is very thorough and has plenty of images.

Teachers are fortunate that there are plenty of films and documentaries available to support the teaching of this topic. Scenes from Ridley Scott's *Gladiator* are very good, while *Spartacus* is another film with good gladiator scenes. The internet is another good source of material. The BBC History website has some very good material on both gladiators and the Colosseum: **http://www.bbc.co.uk/history/ancient/romans**

Teaching suggestions

- It is perhaps hard to make an effective comparison with sports today, but students may like to reflect on the appeal of modern combat sports such as boxing, wrestling and fencing.
- While students will enjoy the glamour of studying the gladiators, it is also important to remember the inhumanity of the Colosseum. You may wish to compare its executions to public executions which exist in parts of the world today. The public cruelty to animals in the Colosseum could of course be paralleled in today's world with bull fighting, bear baiting and circus animals.
- The important social function of the Colosseum was captured in Juvenal's famous disparaging remark about 'bread and circuses' (*Satire* 10.77–81) – the ruling classes kept the masses happy by providing a 'corn dole' for people who did not have enough to eat, and putting on shows to keep them happy. Students may like to consider whether there are modern comparisons with this notion.

A typical day at the races

(Reader, pages 47–49)

This is another popular topic with students. For some background reading, once again Peter Connolly's *The Ancient City* (chapter 9 of Part II) is excellent.

The 'chariot race' from the film *Ben Hur* is the classic film version of this sport. There is plenty of detail in the set for teachers to focus on. For entertaining advice to Roman men about how they should chat up women at the races, Ovid's *Ars Amatoria* I.135–164 is very good and will have the students laughing.

Teaching suggestions

- In terms of modern comparisons, there are clearly plenty of overlaps with horse-racing and motor sport. It is also worth comparing the fanatical support of teams and the idolisation of sporting heroes.
- As above, it is again worth discussing Juvenal's 'bread and circuses' comment in *Satire* 10.

2 Epic and Myth (Unit A352)

Introduction

Whatever other units students have studied, they will have had contact with epic or myth: religious ceremonies, festivals, wall-paintings, education, athletics, drama – wherever they look they see images of gods and heroes and their stories. This unit of the GCSE course allows students to explore one of two vibrant and highly influential works. Students' interest in the classical world often stems from hearing Greek myths as young children, and the opportunity to spend time studying mythology or reading a good adventure story complete with witches and monsters is one they relish. Both the *Odyssey* and the *Metamorphoses* are set outside any defined historical period or social setting, yet reading them imparts much understanding of the values and concerns of all the peoples they are learning about in their other units.

Homer or Ovid? Given that the teacher's enthusiasm is such an important element in successful teaching, the choice is probably down to what the teacher can teach best. The resource implications are the same for both: a copy of the text and (preferably) the Reader to guide students' study in the direction of the specification are the essential equipment. For both texts the emphasis is on a thorough knowledge and understanding of the content and the ability to respond to the themes specified.

The *Odyssey* is essentially a single story with the same hero throughout and with the very strong narrative thread of Odysseus' journey. This means that there are far fewer names and episodes to remember than in the *Metamorphoses*, and the relative simplicity of the narrative may make it more attractive for certain classes. However, overall it is not necessarily easier. Greater depth of character analysis is required, and there are more sustained themes, such as *xenia* and civilisation, to discuss.

If the *Odyssey* is a linear journey, the *Metamorphoses* is a whirlwind through a succession of tales, the characters and mood changing almost by the page. The range of settings, characters, emotions and relationships, not to mention the fantastic metamorphoses, suits very well the lively imagination of many students.

If the teacher is still in doubt about the right option to choose, reading the teaching suggestions in this chapter will help them make a decision.

The CD in the Reader contains several extracts from the texts (see Appendix 1).

Homer, The Odyssey

This option will require candidates to have a detailed knowledge of the set books, and to analyse, evaluate and respond to them in their cultural and literary context.

Homer *The Odyssey*, Books 5, 6, 7, 9, 10 and 12.

Candidates should be able to demonstrate knowledge and understanding of the following:

- Odysseus as a hero
- the role and characterisation of Odysseus, Calypso, Nausicaa, Alcinous, Arete, Polyphemus, the Cyclopes, Circe and Athene
- the presentation of the Sirens, Scylla and Charybdis
- the role of the gods
- the role of women (to include Calypso and Circe as well as the mortal women)
- *xenia* (the guest–host relationship) in the Odyssey
- civilisation and barbarism
- Homer's narrative and descriptive techniques
- Homer as a story-teller and the idea of epic

Key resources

The books on the specification are almost freestanding, the first four books of the epic being concerned mainly with Telemachus' search for his father, and Books 13–24 with his return to Ithaca and revenge on the suitors.

The E. V. Rieu translation (Penguin), with a useful introduction by Peter Jones which contains a summary of all the books, is accessible and has the advantage of being the one that will be used on the examination paper. *Homer's Odyssey: a commentary* by Peter Jones (Bristol Classical Press), based on the English translation of Richmond Lattimore, is an invaluable companion to the Rieu translation as well, both for the teacher and for the more able students.

Jasper Griffin, *Landmarks of World Literature: The Odyssey* (CUP) and W. Camps, *An Introduction to Homer* (OUP) are excellent general introductions to Homer, covering all the aspects on the specification, but written in language generally more suited to an A level student. Martin Thorpe, *Homer* (Bristol Classical Press) is a useful introduction, accessible to GCSE students.

Watching films is generally an effective way of reinforcing a story, but given the liberties that film makers take with the *Odyssey*, it is safer to avoid them. An image on screen can too easily supplant detailed reading of the text in some students' minds. The BBC radio dramatised version (2004) does not have the same pitfalls. Listening to the recording in class and then comparing it with the text can be a useful way of reinforcing knowledge. Michael Wood's *In Search of the Trojan War*, now available as a BBC DVD, contains useful footage of 20th-century bards, and discusses the features of orally transmitted stories.

Aristotle, *Poetics* 24 provides an ancient perspective on epic as a genre. A translation is available at **http://classics.mit.edu/Aristotle/poetics.htm**

The cultural and literary context

There is a very limited amount of background information a teacher can give students, but you might want to respond briefly to their enquiries about Odysseus' route before focusing on the text. They must understand that it is the poem itself that will be the object of their study.

'You will find the route of Odysseus when you find the fellow who sewed up the bag of winds,' said Eratosthenes. However, a map and possible locations might help some students to appreciate the scale of Odysseus' wanderings and to have a context within which to remember his adventures. **http://iam.classics.unc.edu/map/map_idx.html** has maps on which they could plot possible routes. For this purpose, modern names will do: Cicones (Bulgaria); lotus eaters (Libya or Tunisia); Cyclopes (Sicily or near Naples); Aeolus (Lipari or Stromboli); Laestrygonians (Corsica, Sardinia or Sicily); Circe (north of Naples); the Sirens (Gulf of Salerno or Sorrento); Scylla and Charybdis (Straits of Messina); Thrinacia (Sicily); Ogygia (Malta); Scherie (Corfu). They need to know, however, that all this is conjecture, and that Homer himself would have been amalgamating many adventure stories in composing his epic.

It is as impossible to give a precise cultural setting for the *Odyssey* as it is a geographical one. The poem developed orally and will have been continuously modified and updated to the point when Homer made his version. However, there can be little harm in giving students who have no concept at all of 'Homer's world' a glimpse of some artefacts from Bronze Age Greece. The internet can provide ample examples from Mycenae. Try Moses Finley's *The World of Odysseus* (out of print but not difficult to get hold of): though controversial, it is a good starting point. Peter Jones in his introduction to the Penguin translation by Rieu raises some of the problems of Homer and history.

A notion of what an undeveloped Greek island looks like can also help students whose concept of Greece is locked in the 21st century. The difficulty of finding a safe harbour and food for over 700 men whilst travelling across hostile seas is far removed from a GCSE student's experience!

The students need to understand the cultural context of the epic, where travel is unusual, dangerous and difficult; nature and gods are powerful; looking after guests is a social and moral duty, dining and story-telling represent civilised behaviour; telling lies is not frowned upon; and Odysseus' liaisons with Calypso and Circe are not seen as immoral in any way.

The literary context also needs to be emphasised – see page 27 below.

Teaching the story

The Reader gives students guidance on how to approach the elements for study as detailed in the specification. It assumes that the student will already have read the text. Some students encounter considerable difficulty with that first reading. A short exercise to make them rework the story just after they have read it can be a great help in enabling them to retain the content of the narrative. Whilst creative and empathy writing can lead to unreined imagination and be counter-productive, a very structured exercise which requires a reworking of the text can be very useful. The following suggestions of ways to get summaries written include just enough creativity to motivate the average student.

Teaching suggestions

Book 5

- Complete the Mount Olympus Mission Report:

  God on mission: Hermes

  Sent by:

  Purpose:

  Method of transport:

  Route:

  Destination:

  Treatment on arrival:

  Reaction of Circe to the message:

Book 6

- 'She herself retired to her own apartments, where a fire was lit for her' (Book 7, line 6). Imagine you are Nausicaa sitting by that fire. You write a letter to your best friend, telling her about the day's adventure.

(Remind students that there is no evidence of people writing letters (or anything else) in the *Odyssey*.)

Book 7

- You are an estate agent. Write the sales details for the palace of Alcinous.

Book 9

- Write Odysseus' logbook, stating where he stayed, whom he met and why he left.

Book 10

- Compose a brochure for Circe's bed and breakfast establishment, describing the garden, house and furnishings, services available, meals on offer and the charms of the hostess.
- Draw a sketch map of the harbour at Telepylus, showing where the ships were moored.
- Find all the references to people bursting into tears or weeping.

Book 12

- Using Circe's description, draw a picture of Scylla.
- Make a list of the instructions Circe gives to Odysseus, then examine how carefully he follows her instructions.

Students can be helped to focus on the text if they are required to compile a table and fill in the gaps as they read. The exact timing or number of crew may not be important, but the precision involved in carrying out this activity will encourage close reading and help the student to appreciate the order of events. Here are two examples:

Chronology

Book	Time	Events
5	5 days	Mercury arrives, Odysseus builds boat
	18 days	At sea, until Poseidon sees him
	3 days	Leaves raft, swims, arrives at land of Phaeacians

The crew

Book	Crew	Number lost and how
9	12 ships × 60 men = 720	
	648	72 men killed by the Cicones
	642	Cyclops eats 6

Once the text has been read and understood, work can start on the elements mentioned in the specification.

Odysseus as a hero

In the Reader (page 51) students are asked to come up with their own criteria for a hero. Whilst personal response should be encouraged, students must be aware that they cannot blame Homer for creating a character who doesn't fit exactly their preconception of a hero. Discussion of the Homeric view of a hero will help them better to appreciate Odysseus and answer the questions on page 55.

Reputation (the Greek term is *kleos*) is important because your reputation is what lives on after you are dead. In the ancient Greek system of values, it was more important to be seen to be successful than to have any great moral righteousness. This can make the hero appear to students unduly boastful or arrogant. When Odysseus announces that his fame has reached the heavens, he is reinforcing his reputation. Picking out all the instances when those he meets say they have heard of him will help students to appreciate the importance of fame.

Physical appearance and wealth confirm and enhance reputation, hence Odysseus' concern with the gifts he receives. Students might consider today's celebrity culture before they condemn Odysseus for arrogance!

Some students may need no preparation for the essay titles on page 55 of the Reader. For those who need to rehearse the arguments, a variety of activities can be used to explore ideas and examples.

Teaching suggestions

- A formal debate: 'This house believes that Odysseus was a bad leader', for example, can cause students to dredge the text for evidence when their winning or losing the debate is at stake.
- A worksheet which requires matching a statement about his character with a sentence from the text. This clarifies elements

of his character and provides a list of relevant quotations for inclusion in an essay or for revision.

- You are Odysseus. Write a job application in which you have to convince the reader that you are intelligent, a strategic thinker, versatile, resourceful, have good practical skills and can communicate well with people at all levels. (This could equally well be a spoken exercise, with Odysseus delivering a speech on the same lines.)
- You are Eurylochus. You want to get the men on your side. Find every negative point you can with which to blacken Odysseus' character.
- Calypso, Circe and Nausicaa all have fond memories of Odysseus. What did each admire about him?

The more able students will realise that in the books they are studying, Odysseus is telling his own story in public, and they may want to probe the ways in which the hero might have been keen to show himself in a good light in his narrative.

Characterisation

Depth of characterisation comes in the latter part of the epic with Penelope, Telemachus, the servants and the suitors. In our books, we have mostly characters who appear in the *Odyssey* in order to provide Odysseus with an adventure, probably grafted from another story onto the narrative at some time in its organic development. These characters all allow Odysseus to display his personality, and this aspect of their role is a fruitful path for study since it helps students to develop their appreciation of Odysseus himself.

Teaching suggestions

- Students could work their way through the characters on pages 55–63 of the Reader, noting what qualities the hero uses, or has to develop, in dealing with them.

The role of the gods

In the Reader, students are given summaries of the gods as they appear in the books set for study (pages 55–56), but to get an overview, the first line of the poem makes useful reading: 'Tell me, Muse, the story of that resourceful man ...'. Despite the appearance of gods from time to time, the *Odyssey* is very much a story of human behaviour. 'What a lamentable thing it is that men should blame the gods and regard us as the source of their troubles, when it is their own transgressions which bring them suffering that was not their destiny' (Book 1, lines 33–36). Of the crew's destruction, which students read about in Book 12, it is said: 'It was their own transgression that brought them to their doom' (Book 1, line 6). Odysseus himself comments that the counter-attack by the Cicones was a punishment from Zeus for the men's behaviour. Students need to be aware that the gods are not always controlling the events.

Teaching suggestions

- Ask students to go through the story, attributing events either to the will of the gods or the behaviour of man.
- One interesting aspect of Homer's gods and goddesses is that they slip easily between the divine and human worlds. Hermes, for example, flies from Mount Olympus and then on arrival has a nice cup of red nectar before complaining of a boring journey. Ask students to find other examples of this divine/human behaviour mix.

The role of women

We don't meet Penelope in our books, and so goddesses, witches and monsters outnumber the more human women. Any students who want to get a more balanced view might read Book 23, where they will see that Penelope is as quick-witted as her husband. They will also see in her Nausicaa's subservience to the male-dominated domestic order combined with a quiet assertiveness which ensures she gets what she wants.

Teaching suggestions

- In order to clarify the roles of the women characters and record textual evidence for use in essays, such as those on page 60 of the Reader, students can draw up a grid and fill in the details for all the females Odysseus meets:

Page ref	Character	Action	Help or hindrance?

- Those who have studied Athens might like to consider how the females in the *Odyssey* would have been received in 5th-century Athens.
- Speed dating: divide the class into groups of four. Odysseus spends two minutes with each of Nausicaa, Circe and Calypso. Each has to set out her case, using material from the text, that she is the woman who should replace Penelope in his affections.
- Edith Hall discusses women in *The Return of Odysseus* (Tauris) and sees the *Odyssey* as a misogynistic work, with Circe, for example, as the archetypal dangerous woman, and containing the message that female sexuality is dangerous if not controlled within marriage. The more able students might like to consider Edith Hall's thesis. If they do, then they would do well to look also at Penelope in Books 21 and 23.

Xenia (the guest–host relationship)

The Reader explains *xenia* (page 63), but students will not understand its full impact without knowing more about the story. The Trojan War had begun because Paris, the Trojan prince, when invited to the house of Menelaus, broke the rules of *xenia* by stealing his host's wife, Helen. The *Odyssey* ends when Odysseus kills 108 suitors who also have abused *xenia* by taking over his palace and consuming his resources, while hoping to marry his wife.

Teaching suggestions

- Read the account of Telemachus' visit to Menelaus at the beginning of Book 4. From this account, draw up a code for *xenia*.
- As a treat, watch Book 13 onwards on the 1997 film of the *Odyssey* and observe the behaviour of the suitors. Students will also like to compare the film portrayal of Odysseus with their own picture of him.
- Give out a selection of passages from the text with the invitation to guess: Whose home? Which meal? Which bath-time? Whose gift? Having answered the question the student will have a useful list of examples of *xenia* for revision or essay-plan purposes.
- Ask students to compose an entry for a guidebook that advises travellers about what to expect and how to behave, when staying with a stranger in Homer's world.

Civilisation and barbarism

Supplication is related to *xenia* in that supplication happens when one person throws himself on the mercy of another. It is well illustrated in Book 6, lines 139–197 when Odysseus needs Nausicaa's help, and again in Book 7, lines 139–152 when he meets Arete. As Zeus is the god of suppliants, the act has a religious sanctity about it.

Communal eating, drinking wine and feasting on roast meat are associated with civilised behaviour. Clothes, beautiful hair and baths are also appreciated in Homer's world as facets of civilised living.

Teaching suggestions

- Ask students to read what Odysseus says in Book 9, lines 1–11, and then to find as many instances as they can of Odysseus showing pleasure in eating with his companions.

- A comparison between the Cyclops' meals and the meal that Odysseus enjoys at Alcinous' palace will highlight for students the differences between uncivilised and civilised behaviour.

Some parts of the text will raise the question of whether Odysseus always behaves in a civilised way. Students might well question his destroying Ismarus and taking women and vast plunder, or his helping himself to the Cyclops' cheeses.

Homer's narrative and descriptive techniques

When a question asks how a character is portrayed, or why a passage is exciting, or what makes a scene vivid, the student needs to be able to go beyond the narrative content and analyse the style. The following exercises can give them confidence in articulating what many of them may feel intuitively as they read or listen.

Teaching suggestions

- As a first step, give them a passage of 20 or so lines and a list of features of his style – the list in the Reader (pages 64–66) covers the main ones. Ask them to find examples of the features.
- Ask them to listen to passages on the recording. What has stuck in their minds? Why? Help them to shape their spontaneous responses into the language of literary criticism.
- Take a page of text. Using the checklist in the Reader, play the game of ' spot the example' of Homer's descriptive techniques: ten points for a simile, two for an epithet, and so on.
- Ask students in pairs to find a passage of 15 or so lines which they think an examiner could choose to put with the question: 'How does Homer engage the listener in this passage?' They could even write a mark scheme and ask their classmates to answer the question. The discussion thus generated should consolidate their learning about Homer's style.

Homer as story-teller and the idea of epic

In a world where there were no books to read, story-telling was the norm. The bards within the *Odyssey* can be used to explain something of the tradition of story-telling. Look at Demodocus in Book 8, lines 41–109, and Phemis in Book 22, lines 330–371. Insisting that students refer to the text as a poem, not a book, will reinforce the nature of the work.

Teaching suggestions

- Ask students to select an episode which they think would be particularly exciting when recited. They should give reasons why they have chosen it, and say what sort of tone, speed and gestures would be suitable. Some might even be inclined to do a recitation.

Ovid, Metamorphoses

This option will require candidates to have a detailed knowledge of the set books, and to analyse, evaluate and respond to them in their cultural and literary context.

Candidates will be expected to have a detailed knowledge of:

Ovid *Metamorphoses*, Books 1, 3 and 8.

Candidates should be able to demonstrate knowledge and understanding of the following:

- the role and characterisation of Deucalion, Pyrrha, Daphne, Io, Cadmus, Semele, Teiresias, Narcissus, Echo, Pentheus, Minos, Scylla, Daedalus, Meleager, Althaea, Philemon, Baucis and Erysichthon
- the role and character of the gods
- Ovid's portrayal of relationships and emotions
- morality in Ovid's stories
- the idea of metamorphosis
- Ovid's narrative and descriptive techniques

Key resources

The Metamorphoses: a new verse translation by David Raeburn (Penguin Classics), the text which the examiners will use, is accessible. Teachers wanting background reading for Ovid should read L. P. Wilkinson, *Ovid Recalled* (Bristol Classical Press). A hundred pages are dedicated to the *Metamorphoses*, and other chapters are worth reading because the more you know about Ovid's attitude to love and mythology, the better you can appreciate these stories. Those with Latin might also draw on the notes in the texts for the individual books edited by H. E. Gould and J. L. Whiteley (Duckworth), and A. S. Hollis's edition of *Metamorphoses Book 8* (OUP).

There is no social or political background essential to learn for Ovid, no sustained characterisation, no overall plot. The main challenge for the teacher is to help the student remember the large number of names and the range of metamorphoses. Memory for detail is crucial. Most of the advice below, therefore, concentrates on ways to introduce pupils to the text, engage their interest in it and fix the content in their minds.

Teaching the text

The beginning of Book I is probably not the most engaging part of the *Metamorphoses*. It is difficult because of the many names, the abstract nature of it, the lack of dramatic metamorphoses, and the alien subject matter. Given the easy flow and episodic nature of the poem, it's not too much of a crime to start teaching the option with a story that may have more appeal to your class, be it the gory nature of Mars's dragon (not unlike the basilisk in Harry Potter's *Chamber of Secrets*), poor desperate Daphne, or oh-so-vain Narcissus.

The fact that the *Metamorphoses* is a collection of loosely related stories rather than a continuous plot-driven narrative can work in your favour. You can spread the stories over a long period, drip feeding your students to ensure their interest, or even slip in a short one on an impromptu basis when the class is in receptive mood. Capitalise on the lack of grave themes and deep characters to analyse, and go for spontaneous emotion: pity for Echo, indignation at Jupiter's treatment of Io, tears for the fall of Icarus. If they are reacting they have, to a certain extent, got the point. Capitalise, too, on topicality: if there's a local controversy about felling a tree, read Erysichthon; if an obsessed stalker has been in the news, turn to Scylla.

It helps some students to have visual material, and the *Metamorphoses* certainly lends itself to all sorts of representations. Use published illustrations, such as those from the Ovid Project: Metamorphosing the Metamorphoses, the University of Vermont's editions of 17th-century engravings which depict 150 scenes from the *Metamorphoses*, **http://www.uvm.edu/~hag/ovid/**. See also **www.latein-pagina.de/ovid/ovid_m1.htm** which contains illustrations for *Metamorphoses* 1, from 16th-century manuscripts to Dali and Picasso. A Google image search will provide many other pictures.

Teaching suggestions

- Some students might be inspired to produce their own illustrations: anything from a painting or sculpture which could double up as Art coursework, to stick-men cartoons. Drawings could be passed round, with students having to tell each other the story which corresponds to the picture.
- Designate a small notice board area as your Metamorphosis Collage. Challenge everyone to stick something on and give an explanation to the class of its relevance. This will act as constant revision and also make a good talking point for open days on the relevance of Classical Civilisation.
- Create an Ovid Box containing: a stone, a bay leaf, a purple hairpiece, a cow from a toy farm, a peacock feather, a piece of thread, gold, silver, a bottle of water, a wolf, pine needles, an arrow etc. You pull an object out of the box, and the first one to be able to tell the story it relates to gets ... whatever bribe you use!
- Written summaries are useful for consolidating knowledge and revision. Students can construct a grid to help them remember the actions of the gods, and later to analyse their behaviour:

Page ref	Name of deity	Action	Comments

- Set up a word-search grid and ask the students to copy down the answers next to the clue. That way, when students have finished they will have a list of material to learn and use in their written work. For example, for Book 1 the clues could be: River round the underworld; Mountain where the gods live; Jupiter's weapon; Before creation; Moon goddess; Changed into a wolf; Goddess of the ocean; Pyrrha's husband; The method Jupiter uses to destroy the earth; Name of the sea-green merman.
- Some episodes lend themselves to particular types of aide-mémoire, for example: a series of drawings to show the process of creation; a spidergram to show how Minos links the stories in Book 8; Cadmus' family tree.
- The Reader includes recorded extracts. Help the students to make the most of them by giving them things to do: Listen to an extract and then write down all the names mentioned in it; Write up a story from memory as a newspaper article; Listen to a story every day and then retell it to whoever is with you; Dramatise the story, putting on appropriate voices for each character; Stop the recording mid-story and see if you can finish it, getting as close to Ovid's words as possible.

The characters

As there is no sustained characterisation, it will be important for students to be able to recall under pressure many different characters and relationships across the range of stories.

Teaching suggestions

- The first step could be done in the style of a pub quiz. 'Round One: Fathers and Daughters. 1. Name a girl whose father is a river. 2. Which father exploits his daughter's talents?' And so on. Students could discuss appropriate headings for each round, and then set questions for each other.
- A more demanding exercise, and one better done in writing, would be to ask the student to match the characters to the relationship. This exercise will introduce less able students to descriptive phrases they could draw on in other contexts. For example: a married couple who are devoted to each other; the wife who is touchingly impressed by her husband's intelligence; a woman who is torn by her loyalty to different members of her family.

Students will have to be able to write character sketches. The following exercises will encourage them to look at the physical and psychological attributes.

Teaching suggestions

- You are a Hollywood casting director. Whom would you choose to play the roles of Echo, Narcissus, Erysichthon, Jupiter, Juno and Scylla, and why?
- On page 76 of the Reader, students are asked why Narcissus is so realistic. Go through the other stories looking for character types who are recognisable today (Erysichthon the heartless property developer; Jupiter the serial adulterer; Scylla the obsessed young girl). Soaps and the tabloids might yield some ideas. This will also help in answering questions such as: How do you account for Ovid's continuing popularity?

The role and character of the gods

Ask students to write a list of what comes into their minds when the term 'gods' is mentioned, and they might come up with something like this: 'They are very moral; they always do what is right; they give human beings rules to live by; humans should love and respect them; they care for humans; human beings show them respect by worshipping them; they are honest; they don't have weaknesses in character as humans do.'

The nature of Roman gods is very different: they are powerful, and are worshipped through fear, not love; they often act in an immoral way; they provide no moral code by which humans should live; worship is a question of the correct ritual; to offend a god can be fatal. Making this clear to students will give them some criteria by which to consider the gods in Ovid. The Reader gives an outline of Roman religion (pages 38–42) and points out the importance of ritual and the contractual nature of the Romans' relationship with their gods.

Alongside the great gods of Olympus was the idea of *numina*, the powers that were present in places or objects. Water is very precious, particularly in hot Mediterranean countries, and so rivers and streams were often thought to be inhabited by holy powers. Looking at some old countryside festivals might help students to see how the forces of nature and religion are linked. Ovid's *Fasti*, a calendar of Roman festivals, describes how these countryside deities are worshipped. There is an online translation at **www.tonykline.co.uk**

Teaching suggestions

- Explore these festivals, as described in Ovid's Fasti: Anna Perenna (15 March) – the goddess was worshipped in a sacred grove at a festival which, with its drinking, singing, drunken dancing and improvised tents, has something of the Glastonbury Festival about it; the Terminalia (23 February) – a country festival when families held a sacrifice at the boundary stone; the Fordicidia (15 April) – at this festival the innards of a pregnant cow were sacrificed on the advice of Egeria, a water nymph with a shrine near Rome.
- Students can then identify places described in the *Metamorphoses* which seem to have a numen, or special atmosphere.

Ovid's portrayal of relationships and emotions

One of the elements that binds the stories together is the family relationships and the strong emotions stirred up when there is conflict within a family. Teachers familiar with Greek tragedy will appreciate the influence of Euripides particularly. See page 31 below for resonances in the Scylla story.

Empathy and creative writing can create more misconceptions than understanding, but a short exercise with very specific terms of reference can be an effective way of reinforcing facts and clarifying ideas. Questions such as the ones below force students to write succinctly and coherently about characters and their emotions.

Teaching suggestions

- What are Daphne's thoughts as she is chased by Apollo?
- What would Io have said to her father if she had been able to speak?

- Write Juno's diary (or blog) recounting who her husband is having an affair with, what tricks he has played to get his way and most importantly, how she has got her revenge on him.
- Write a gossip column story on the behaviour and attitude of Narcissus.
- Write a lonely hearts column entry, for example: 'Romantic girl sensitive to music willing to murder for heroic husband'.

Morality in Ovid's stories

The Reader helps students to identify the reasons for the characters' metamorphoses and discusses those who are punished for a crime (see pages 70–76). But did Ovid mean his readers to learn any lessons from the tales? He does comment on the injustice of Actaeon's punishment, and we are left to infer that the gods behave like spoilt children.

One of the main causes of distress for females in the *Metamorphoses* is Jupiter. Students are likely to condemn his behaviour. However, a read of Ovid's *Amores* or the *Ars Amatoria* (available online as above) will show that the persona of the poet too devoted much of his time to seducing young women.

Teaching suggestions

- 'The fact that Actaeon devoted his life to hunting did not prevent Diana from destroying him. So Ovid's message must be that there is no point in worshipping the gods.' Ask students to apply this assertion to other stories to see if it holds true for them too.
- Students could discuss whether they think that Ovid criticises Jupiter for his crimes, or treats his sexual adventures as good sport, and his victims as fair game.

The idea of metamorphosis

Students can be reminded that metamorphosis is not restricted to ancient poetry.

Teaching suggestions

- Ask them to think about metamorphosis in stories they know, and they should be able to come up with a range from films they may have seen such as *Shrek* or *Beauty and the Beast*, to traditional tales such as those of werewolves or the selkie. More serious works like *Frankenstein*, *Dr Jekyll and Mr Hyde* or even Kafka's *Metamorphoses* or *The Portrait of Dorian Gray* could be brought to their attention. They could then consider why metamorphosis is such a popular theme, and whether the creators of these stories were conveying any message through the metamorphosis.
- In the Reader (pages 70–76), students are given a list of various reasons for metamorphosis. Ask them to discuss how they would categorise the metamorphoses of the following: the blood of Mother Earth's offspring; the stones thrown by Deucalion and Pyrrha; Io; Teiresias; the teeth of the dragon; Juno; Echo; Narcissus; the sailors; Nisus; Ariadne's crown; Perdix; Meleager's sisters; Perimele; Acheolous.

Ovid's narrative and descriptive techniques

The Reader (pages 81–86) gives a list of the main features of Ovid's style. They can be made into a checklist for students to apply as they answer source-based questions.

Teaching suggestions

- Give each student a story, with the instruction to present to the class the narrative techniques that Ovid has used in that story.
- In order to appreciate Scylla's rhetoric and be familiar with something which Ovid's Roman audience would have known well, read the *Aeneid*, Book 4, lines 365–387 (Dido berates Aeneas for leaving her); Euripides, *Hippolytus*, lines 350–451 (the nurse convinces Phaedra that her love should be acted upon); and Euripides, *Medea*, lines 465–497 (Medea reminds Jason what she has done for him).

The Reader (page 67) asks the student to imagine Ovid's poetry being recited after dinner as entertainment. Encourage the students to identify what makes the stories so entertaining by giving them one of the following exercises.

Teaching suggestions

- Imagine you are a film director. You can choose one story to put on film. Which would you choose and why?
- You have to write in 300 words the publicity material for a new edition of Ovid's *Metamorphoses* which the publisher hopes will become a bestseller. Say why the stories are essential reading.
- Make a PowerPoint presentation of the way Ovid links the stories together.

3 Community Life in the Classical World (Unit A353)

Introduction

Both Sparta and Pompeii are unique fields of study in the classical world, although for very different reasons. Sparta was a society completely different to any other in the Greek world; a military state, it was successful on the back of the mass enslavement of peoples in the neighbouring regions. The lack of first hand evidence about the city means that it retains an air of mystery which is unlikely ever to be lifted. Pompeii, on the other hand, is the society from the classical world about which we have the most first hand evidence. The nature of its destruction in volcanic ash and lava means that we are able to construct with some accuracy what life was like at the time that the town was destroyed.

Unlike with the 'Athens or Rome' choice in the City Life unit, there are few areas of overlap between the Sparta and Pompeii options. Both are fascinating, but offer very different experiences for the student.

The main area of similarity is that both options partly focus on one moment in history, each of which has a profound effect on the respective city. In the Sparta option, this is of course the story surrounding the battle of Thermopylae, for which there is the detailed written evidence of the historian Herodotus, as well as the geographical evidence of the battlefield. In the Pompeii option, this is the tale of the eruption of Vesuvius in 79 AD, which led to the destruction of the city. As with Thermopylae, there is an important historical account (by Pliny) about this dramatic event. Therefore, in both options, students will have the opportunity to read a contemporary account about the society they are studying.

Moreover, both options allow students to reflect on the importance of archaeological evidence, albeit from very different perspectives: in Sparta, it is hard to know how helpful the very limited archaeological evidence is; in Pompeii, the issue is how best to preserve and protect the vast quantities of such evidence.

Sparta is distinct even from any other city in the Greek world. In fact, its very appeal is how different it is from any other society in the classical world. Sparta was unique in its education system, its treatment of women, the military lifestyle lived by its citizens, and the amount and nature of the slave labour used to maintain its success. These issues allow students and teachers to examine wider issues of education, the position of women in society, the treatment of slaves and militarism, through the prism of Spartan life. The Sparta option requires detailed focus on Herodotus' account of the battle of Thermopylae; students who are particularly interested in ancient military tactics will particularly enjoy this element of the course.

One of the appeals of the Pompeii option is that it allows students to examine an ancient town as it was in Roman times and as it is now as a major archaeological site. There are plenty of issues to discuss surrounding good practice and ethics in archaeology, as well as the preservation of ancient sites in conjunction with modern tourism. Unlike Sparta, Pompeii gives the student a chance to examine domestic and home life in close detail through the study of two of the most famous houses in Pompeii. Finally, Pompeii is of course a superb option if you are planning a school Classics trip to the Bay of Naples – you really can go and examine in detail what you are studying.

As mentioned in the introduction to the City Life unit, you may wish to tie in your choice with the other units you are teaching. It is true to say that Athens and Sparta go together very well as options, since the two co-existing societies are so different and can be contrasted in many areas (e.g. the education of children, the treatment of women). Likewise, Rome and Pompeii complement each other well – the former looks at the capital city of the empire, while the latter offers a window into the everyday life of a provincial town in that empire.

Even if you decide to stick with two Greek or two Roman options in these areas, it is important to remember that each of the two literature options is compatible with either Greek or Roman options. For the Romans, Greek works of literature such as Homer's *Odyssey* were central to their culture and education, while Ovid's *Metamorphoses* sees a Roman author recounting myths which are predominantly Greek. Once again, it is also worth suggesting that students actually enjoy some exposure to both the Greeks and the Romans.

Both options are well resourced by books and the internet, although inevitably there is more visual information about Pompeii, as well as plenty of documentaries about the city and its destruction. However, there is also plenty of material about the Spartans and particularly the battle of Thermopylae (not least the recent film *300*, which shouldn't be treated as gospel fact!). In short, both options offer a great deal in terms of resources but Pompeii has a seemingly endless supply.

Sparta

The focus of this option is the unique social, political and military organisation of Sparta.

Candidates will be expected to have an understanding of the ethos of the Spartans and how such attitudes were encouraged and maintained in Sparta. Candidates should also be aware of the content and difficulties of assessing the value of non-Spartan sources on Spartan life.

Some Spartan history should be studied in order to see Sparta acting as a military force in keeping with its ideals and goals.

The Spartan state	The geographical position of Sparta in Greece. Details of her policy towards and conquest of Messenia.
Sparta and other Greeks	The nature and limitations of the evidence: Aristophanes, Xenophon and Plutarch on women and education. Aristotle on education and government. Spartan attitudes to non-Spartans. Sparta's isolationism and the attitudes of other Greeks towards Sparta.
Social structure	The *Spartiatai*, the *Periokoi* (origins) and the Helots (origins). The different duties and roles of each class. The concept of *Eunomia.*
Culture/artistic achievements	Poetry (the nature of the content of the poems of Tyrtaios), bronze works, sculpture and pottery.
Government	Eligibility, election, duties, responsibilities and limitations of: the Kings; the *Gerousia* the *Ephors*; the *Ecclesia (Apella).*
Lykourgos	The legend of his establishment as a leader in Sparta. His contribution to education in Sparta.
Education of boys	The purpose of the *agoge.* The treatment of boys, from birth to joining the military messes. Games, discipline, food, clothing, organisation (platoons, *eirenes*). The role of the *paidonomos.*
Women	Their upbringing, marriage, daily life, physical appearance, duties and land holding. Attitude of other Greeks.
Military organisation	The army's organisation and fighting methods. Training, appearance and equipment (particularly based on statuary), accommodation. The *syssitia, krypteia.*
The Spartan army in action	An understanding of the basic facts on the heroism of Leonidas and the 300. Candidates should be aware of the basic details of the account in Herodotus: *Histories,* Book VII, Chapters 207 to the end, including the role and influence of Demaratus.

Key resources

If teachers are looking for some background reading about Spartan society, then Paul Cartledge's *The Spartans: An Epic History* (Channel 4 Books) gives a good overview of its history. For a detailed explanation of the development of Spartan society, chapter 3 of Tom Holland's *Persian Fire* (Abacus) is thorough and well sourced. Anton Powell's *Athens and Sparta* (Routledge) gives a detailed and scholarly account of Spartan society and its relationship with Athens. Chapter 6 of James Renshaw's *In Search of the Greeks* (Bristol Classical Press) gives a clear and detailed account of the material required for the specification, together with a number of key maps and images; this can also be used by students.

As Sparta is an option with a limited range of original sources, teachers will find it well worth familiarising themselves with two of the main primary sources on the city-state: Plutarch's *Life of Lykourgos* (alternatively spelt as 'Lycurgus'), an online version of which is available at **http://penelope.uchicago.edu/Thayer/E/Roman/Texts/Plutarch/Lives/Lycurgus*.html** The other main source is Xenophon's *Spartan Society*. Both of these important texts can be found in *Plutarch: On Sparta* (Penguin Classics).

For teaching purposes, the Ancient History Sourcebook has some good material on Sparta: **http://www.fordham.edu/halsall/ancient/asbook07.html#Sparta**. Another excellent resource is the Channel 4 documentary series *The Spartans*, presented by Bettany Hughes. This is available on DVD and is well worth investing in if you are going to teach the option.

The Spartan state, Lykourgos, culture/artistic achievements

(Reader, pages 88–92)

It is probably worth teaching the development of Spartan society (involving both 'the Spartan state' and 'Lykourgos' in the specification) alongside the 'culture/artistic achievements' aspect, since Spartan culture and artistic achievements really belong to its earlier history. Pages 223–232 of *In Search of the Greeks* has a clear outline of the history and geography of Sparta, as well as briefly examining its cultural and artistic achievements; it then leads on to describing the figure of Lykourgos.

Teaching suggestions

- It is important for students to start out with a clear idea of the geographical location of Sparta, Laconia and Messenia. Giving them an outline map of Greece to label is probably essential. *In Search of the Greeks* has a variety of maps of Sparta and its place in the Peloponnese and the rest of Greece. The following website has a range of outline maps: **http://iam.classics.unc.edu/map/map_idx.html**
- As with other options, students might be encouraged to draw up a brief timeline of Spartan history.
- The figure of Lykourgos is a mysterious one. Students could be asked to think about other 'founding fathers' and what they tell us about that country (King Arthur and William Tell are two good examples). Plutarch is the main source for Lykourgos, but it is also worth reading Herodotus' account of his visit to the Delphic oracle at *Histories* 1.65. Lykourgos' role in developing the education system is mentioned below under 'Education of boys'.
- A website with a decent range of samples of early Spartan artwork is **http://www.sikyon.com/sparta/Art/sparta_peg01.html**
- The wars with Messenia are the best time to introduce the poetry of Tyrtaios. There is plenty of scope here to compare his work with other war literature – the poetry of the First World War is an obvious point of comparison. Students could look at John McCrae's patriotic 'In Flanders Fields' and compare it with a more lamenting poem, such as Wilfred Owen's 'Dulce et Decorum

Est'. Which of the two can be most closely compared to Tyrtaios?

- It is also worth looking more closely at one of Tyrtaios' poems, some of which can be found at **http://www.spartan-world.de/tyrtaeus2_text.html**. Diehl[3] 1.1.9, for example, has plenty of interesting material (see Appendix 2).

Sparta and other Greeks

(Reader, pages 90–91, 102)

Sparta was a city state which chose to live in isolation from the other Greek cities. As a result, it was something of a mystery to other Greeks, and one to be feared due to its military prowess. In some ways, it could be compared with the communist countries of the 'iron curtain' in 20th-century Europe – people were prevented from leaving or entering, while the style of living in Sparta was radically different to elsewhere in the Greek world. A good summary of the relationship between Sparta and the outside world can be found on pages 266–267 of *In Search of the Greeks*.

Sparta could not have been more different from its great rival in the Greek world, Athens, a city which encouraged immigration, enterprise and democracy. A very good starting point for understanding how the Athenians compared themselves to the Spartans can be found in Thucydides' account of Pericles' funeral speech in his *History of the Peloponnesian War* (2.34–46). This was delivered by the Athenian general at a mass funeral to commemorate the war dead in 430 BC, at the end of the first year of the war between the two cities. It is of course a very Atheno-centric view of the two societies, but a very interesting insight into how the differences between the two cities were probably perceived. It is certainly worth a teacher reading it, and it would provide excellent extension for a bright and well motivated class.

Of course, it is much harder to know what the Spartans thought about the Athenians (or other Greeks) simply because they have produced no written records at all as a society, apart from the early poetry of Tyrtaios (and two other early lyric poets – Alcman and Terpander – who tell us little of day to day life in Sparta). This is one of the great problems of Spartan society – all of our sources are from non-Spartans; moreover, most of them were either ill-informed or biased against the city. For an analysis of the main sources available to us on Sparta, see pages 232–233 of *In Search of the Greeks*.

The specification requires students to be familiar with 'Aristophanes, Xenophon and Plutarch on women and education' and 'Aristotle on education and government'. Discussion of the relevant passages from these authors can be found below under 'Women', 'Education of boys' and 'Government'.

Teaching suggestions

- Students could be encouraged to think about the objectivity of historical sources and perhaps reflect how sure we can be about the nature of Spartan society. There is great scope here to extend the discussion to thinking about how we know about the past; moreover, will the advent of modern technology such as email and internet make it much easier for future generations to have a greater idea about what 'everyday life' was like in our society?
- Again, it is a good idea to get students to make modern comparisons. Can they think of modern societies or countries who are deeply suspicious of one another because they have different beliefs about how to live? Can this be compared to the relationship between Athens and Sparta?

Social structure (Reader, pages 92–94)

This is a relatively straightforward topic to teach. For background information, see pages 235–238 of *In Search of the Greeks*.

Teaching suggestions

- Students could think about whether people are born into roles in societies today. Does the class system still exist in this country? More extreme examples might be the former apartheid regime in South Africa or the caste system in India.
- There is an opportunity to compare the types of slavery in the ancient world. Under either the 'Athens' or 'Rome' option, students will study a more 'traditional' form of slavery, and it would be worth them comparing this with the lives of the helots.
- The treatment of the helots by Spartiatai also opens the door for teachers to discuss issues such as bullying, human rights and the dehumanisation of enemies. There are clearly many comparisons to be made with the modern world here.

Government (Reader, pages 99–102)

Aristotle (384–322 BC), who came from northern Greece but lived much of his life at Athens, wrote a long treatise, *Politics*, which examined various political systems throughout the Greek world. These systems were fundamentally split into four categories: monarchy, oligarchy, tyranny and democracy.

At various points in *Politics* Aristotle makes mention of the Spartan constitution; his main criticisms are summarised between 1270b and 1271a, where, amongst other things, he complains that the system of election for the Gerousia is 'childish' and that the members of the Gerousia are liable to becoming old, out of touch and even senile. Earlier in *Politics*, at 1265b, he assesses how the Spartan constitution is perceived by other Greeks:

'There are indeed some who say that the best constitution is one composed of a mixture of all types, and who therefore praise the Spartan. Some of these say that it is made up out of oligarchy, monarchy and democracy: its kingship is monarchy, the authority of the Gerousia is oligarchy, and yet it is also run democratically through the authority exercised by the Ephors, who come from the people. Others say that the Ephorate is a tyranny, and that the democratic element is to be found in the common meals and the other features of daily life.' (trans: Sinclair)

In addition to Aristotle, we have important information about the Kings at Sparta in Herodotus' *Histories* 6.56–60.

Teaching suggestions

- One of the main areas to examine in this topic is the nature of the checks and balances between each of the four sections of government. The concept of a dual kingship is rare in the ancient world (although the consuls in Rome are another example), and ensured that no one individual became too powerful; the Ephors were powerful but only in power for one year; the Gerousia possibly had the most influence; while although the Ecclesia had little power, they represented 'public opinion' in Sparta and elected the members of the Gerousia and the Ephors from their number.
- To read an account of a meeting of the Ecclesia in action, Thucydides (1.79–88) describes a debate about whether to go to war with Athens.
- Note that the assembly is known as the Ecclesia. In the past, it has also been known as the Apella (the name in parentheses on the specification rubric), although this has now shown to be incorrect. However, many older textbooks will still refer to the Apella.

Education of boys (Reader, pages 94–96)

The main sources on Spartan education are Plutarch (*Life of Lykourgos* 16–18) and Xenophon (*Spartan Society* 2–4), while Aristotle (*Politics* 1338b) is critical of the fact that Spartan education focused exclusively on producing physical courage, to the exclusion of all other qualities:

'The Spartans ... by severity of exercise render (their boys) like wild animals, under the impression that this is particularly conducive to courage ... Those who permit their young to indulge in excessive physical training, leaving them without education in essentials, are effectively turning them into machines ...' (trans: Sinclair)

Teaching suggestions

- Two obvious points of comparison are with the education which students receive today and with the education system they study in either the 'Athens' or the 'Rome' option. Teachers might want to raise the question, 'What makes for a good education?'
- There is also scope with this topic to research and discuss infanticide in the world today: in many parts of the developing world, boys are still more highly valued than girls. It also touches on the debate about genetic selection – should a parent be able to choose the gender of a child? Teachers might wish to research Hitler's attitude to disabled children, since he was apparently influenced by the Spartan policy in this area.
- This topic also opens the way for discussion of bullying of younger children by older children at school, and perhaps ties in with the Victorian public school world described in *Tom Brown's Schooldays.*

Women (Reader, pages 102–104)

This is another fascinating topic which is likely to provoke lively debate. The key sources are Plutarch (*Life of Lykourgos* 14–15) and Xenophon (*Spartan Society* 1), while it is also worth looking at the *Sayings of Spartan Women*, which can be found in the Penguin Classic edition *Plutarch: On Sparta*. For an alternative view, Aristotle is scathing in his view of Spartan women in *Politics* 1269b–1270a.

An amusing portrayal of Spartan women is given by the Athenian comic playwright Aristophanes in his play *Lysistrata*, which was produced in 411 BC at the height of the 27 year war between the two cities and their respective allies. It is important to be aware that Aristophanes was a satirist who was writing to make people laugh; no doubt he did this by playing on stereotypes. We should be very careful, then, not to assume that his plays represent historical accuracy. However, it is also fair to say that stereotypes need some basis in truth in order to be funny.

Lysistrata is a play about the women of Athens and Sparta, and in particular about an Athenian woman, Lysistrata, who is fed up with her husband always being away at war. She gathers together a conference of women from all the cities involved in the war and proposes that they should all stage a 'sex strike' until their men agree to stop the war. Clearly, this is a play with plenty of comic potential! At the conference, a woman from Sparta called Lampito turns up (lines 77–84), and she is portrayed as a fit, athletic and no-nonsense woman. It is well worth reading these lines with your students.

Teaching suggestions

- It is essential to compare Spartan women with women elsewhere in the ancient world – students will either study Athenian women or Roman women in the City Life unit of the specification. Students should be encouraged to realise just how different and novel was the lifestyle of the women of Sparta.
- You may wish to pose the question, 'Was Sparta an early feminist state?' The answer is probably not, since women were really baby machines of the state, but the relative freedoms and education given to Spartan women neatly leads into a discussion about what constitutes 'feminism'.
- Students might also consider the politics of sex. In most ancient societies, men were obsessed by ensuring the paternity of their children by preventing their wives from having contact with other men. In Sparta, this problem is removed by their different

sexual customs, and this in turn gave more freedom to women.

- You might hand out some of the sayings of Spartan women and ask your students to use them to come up with a description of a conversation or interview with a Spartan woman.

Military organisation and the Spartan army in action (Reader, pages 96–99)

These two topics are clearly at the heart of Spartan society. An excellent book on all things military in Sparta is *The Spartan Army* by Nick Sekunda (Osprey); this also includes many images and reconstructions of Spartan military matters. Chapter 7 of Tom Holland's *Persian Fire* gives a detailed description of the battle of Thermopylae and is good background reading for a teacher, as are pages 90–99 of Paul Cartledge's *The Spartans: An Epic History*, which give a detailed biography of Demaratus. Pages 253–260 of *In Search of the Greeks* covers all the material required in the specification.

Of the original sources, chapter 12 of Plutarch's *Life of Lykourgos* describes the *syssitia*, while chapter 22 discusses the Spartans at war and chapter 28 the *Krypteia*. Xenophon goes into great detail about military matters in chapters 11–13 of *Spartan Society*.

Teaching suggestions

- You may invite your students to compare the Spartan army with a modern professional army, particularly in its attitude to training and the use of messes to build team spirit.
- When dealing with the *Krypteia*, there is scope to raise the question of why young men are often the most prone to violence and fanaticism – there are clearly resonances here with society today.
- The *syssitia* were a way of pursuing equality – by dining together, people were united and there was no difference in the quality and amount of food they ate. What modern ways are used to try to break down social and generational differences?
- The battle of Thermopylae is clearly a very engaging topic, and there is plenty of material on the internet to support your teaching of it. You could ask students to write an account of the battle as if they were present. The film *300* is well worth a look at this point, although you might want to get your students to write down all the historical inaccuracies as they watch it!
- For any students who are particularly keen on the topic, Valerio Massimo Manfredi's novel *Spartan* is an exciting account of Spartan life at the time of Thermopylae.

Pompeii

The focus of this unit is the study of Pompeii as a unique source for our understanding of everyday life in a prosperous town at the height of the Roman Empire.

In studying the individual aspects of Pompeii, candidates will be expected to assess the evidence provided by the town and to draw conclusions about its prosperity, the values and priorities of its citizens and the attractiveness of living in such a town. Candidates should recognise how life in Pompeii reflects the success of the Roman empire as a whole.

Candidates will also be expected to understand how the nature of Pompeii's destruction was a key factor in its preservation and thereby its value as an archaeological site.

The original site	Its advantages as a place for settlement.
Destruction	The earthquake of 62 AD and volcanic activity immediately prior to 79 AD. The events of 24–26 August 79 AD; including the substances that buried Pompeii. Pliny as a source. Evidence of how the inhabitants died. The contribution of Giuseppe Fiorelli to the excavation.
Houses	The town house (*domus*) – typical design, layout, main rooms, decoration and furniture – with particular reference to: (a) the House of the Vettii, (b) the House of the Faun. The owners, the layout, particular rooms of special interest, decoration, unusual features, objects found, mosaics and wall paintings; and how the houses reflected the tastes, values and wealth of their owners.
The forum	The layout and the main buildings and their positions: commercial buildings - Macellum, Eumachia, Weights and Measures office, granaries (*horrea*); religious buildings - Temples of Jupiter/Apollo/Emperor (*Lares*); political buildings - offices of the *aediles* and *duovirs*, Basilica, Comitium. Graffiti, statues of leading Pompeians, porticoes, stalls. The importance of the forum as a commercial, political, administrative, social and religious centre.
Government	The town council and magistrates. The duties and responsibilities of *decurions, duovirs* and *aediles*. Guilds and elections; political graffiti, election posters.
Inns and *thermopolia*	Layout, evidence for types of food and drink sold, with specific reference to the Thermopolium of Asellina.
The theatre	The Large Theatre: size, design, including stage and scenery. Comedies and their production in Plautus' time: typical plots and types of character, use of masks. Audience attitudes to shows in the theatres, their involvement and comfort.

The baths	Candidates should have detailed knowledge of the Stabian Baths including: typical features, the layout, the heating system, the bathing experience (*apodyterium, palaestra, tepidarium, caldarium, frigidarium*), other amenities. The baths in relation to the climate, daily routine, business and social life of the Pompeians.
The amphitheatre	The building and the layout, the shows, their purposes, the riot of 59 AD and its consequences.

Key resources

When teaching Pompeii, there are some key resources which should help any teacher. Peter Connolly's book *Pompeii* (OUP) is informative and has numerous fine drawings and illustrations reconstructing life in the town. *The Complete Pompeii* by Joanne Berry (Thames and Hudson) is an excellent though slightly more scholarly companion for teachers learning about the topic. For a collection of ancient sources on the town, *Pompeii: a sourcebook* by A. Cooley and M. Cooley (Routledge) is excellent.

The Pompeii option is also well serviced by teaching software and websites. **http://www.pompeii.co.uk/** gives details about Pompeii Interactive, a CD ROM with plenty of electronic resources about the town. In addition, **http://pompeya.desdeinter.net/pompeya.htm** and **http://www.pompeiisites.org/** have detailed information and resources. **http://www.capware.it/** has a very good series of reconstructions.

The original site (Reader, pages 105–106)

Pompeii did not start its life as a Roman town. Indeed, it did not come under full Roman control until 89 BC, some seven centuries after the settlement was founded. One of the most interesting and formative features of Pompeii is its contact with various cultures: Oscan, Greek, Etruscan, Samnite and Roman. Clearly, its success and development as a town was heavily influenced by its location; the fact that it was set in a fertile landscape and near the sea meant that it was always likely to be influenced by various different cultures, and this remained so throughout the life of the town. Hellenised Egypt was a particular influence, as can be seen from works of art such as the Nile creatures mosaic in the House of the Faun and the popularity of the cult of the goddess Isis.

The history of Pompeii can be divided into two periods: before and after being given Roman colony status in 80 BC. For a detailed description of the theories about Pompeii before Roman colonisation, chapter 3 of *The Complete Pompeii* has an excellent outline.

A defining moment in the history of Pompeii came with the Social Wars of the early 1st century BC. Pompeii, which until this period had been an ally and associate of Rome, broke with its traditional loyalty to its master and joined other Italian cities who were fighting for Roman citizenship. In 89 BC, Pompeii was attacked and conquered by the Roman general Sulla. As a result, Pompeii was turned into a Roman colony in 80 BC, and a full-scale Romanisation took place. Some of the main features of this Romanisation were as follows:

- Many Roman veterans were moved into the city, taking power and influence from the noble Samnite families;
- Latin became the official language of Pompeii (replacing Oscan);
- The Roman system of local government was imposed on the city;
- The amphitheatre was built in 80 BC;
- Two new baths complexes were built – the Forum Baths and Central Baths;
- More luxury houses were built, while Roman villas emerged outside the city walls, such as the Villa of the Mysteries;

- The Forum took on the appearance of a fully Roman forum, with the Temple of Jupiter at its heart, as well as temples to the Emperor and the public Lares;
- During the age of Augustus, the building of the aqueduct brought a fully functioning running water supply to Pompeii for the first time.

Despite this upheaval, Pompeii managed to retain its ability to adapt with the times and remained a cosmopolitan city. The increasing access to Roman trade routes brought more commerce and contact with varied cultures into the city. For example, there is much evidence that the cult of Isis from Egypt was very popular. In addition, after a couple of generations, the 'Roman Pompeians' and 'Samnite Pompeians' had intermarried and Pompeii remained a town of social mobility and the place for entrepreneurs to seek a fortune. As a result, it had a very high percentage of freedmen among its population.

After Augustus became the first Roman Emperor in 30 BC, the era of the Pax Romana (Peace in the Roman Empire) emerged; this greater security meant that Pompeii no longer needed to worry about warfare and was able to enjoy a golden age from the time of Augustus until the earthquake of 62 AD. Evidence of this sense of security can be seen in the fact that housing started to develop on what were previously fortified city walls. In addition, public buildings were enlarged and refaced with marble and there were new statues erected in public meeting places.

Although students do not need to know the information contained above, it makes some sense to start the option by giving them some sense of the history of the town. It is also worth introducing it in conjunction with the material in the Reader on the settlement of Pompeii.

Teaching suggestions

- For a general historical outline, you could hand out a timeline based on the information above (although remember that students need to learn only the dates listed in the specification). In particular, you could examine the increased Roman influence after 80 BC.
- To give students a geographical context, it is worth handing out two maps – one of the Bay of Naples region in Roman times, showing the location of Pompeii in relation to other towns and sites in the region (there is a good – if small – map on page 7 of *Pompeii: a sourcebook*); and an outline map of the city, on which students can mark the main landmarks: the forum, the amphitheatre, the baths, the theatres, etc.
- There is one very important ancient piece of evidence for how the Pompeians saw the mountain which stood near their town. A fresco from the House of the Centenary (which can be viewed at **http://pompeya.desdeinter.net/CasadelCentenario-P-MAN-0038.htm**) shows the god Bacchus beside a mountain which is teeming with symbols of fertility – animals, vegetation and grapes (it was an important wine growing region). Students may wish to reflect on the optimistic nature of this image given what they know about the subsequent eruption of the volcano.

Destruction (Reader, pages 106–108)

This is clearly a very exciting topic, for which there are a great deal of teaching materials. Chapter 1 of *The Complete Pompeii* has some excellent background information.

There is some good material about the earthquake in Pompeii at this site: **http://www.bbc.co.uk/history/ancient/romans/pompeii_portents_01.shtml** (NB some sources give the date of the earthquake as 63 AD rather than 62 AD, as it is disputed by ancient sources. Our specification goes with 62 AD). In addition, students will benefit from looking at the relief panel from the House of Caecilius Iucundus, which depicts the eruption in the forum. Pages 236–241 of *The Complete Pompeii* has a detailed analysis of the earthquake.

There are two good documentaries which deal with the eruption. *Pompeii: the last day* (BBC) and *Secrets of the Dead: the riddle of Pompeii* (Channel 4) are both frequently shown on documentary channels. The former is a dramatised documentary reconstructing the events of the city's final hours, while the latter is a documentary which examines how people died in the eruption.

The history of the excavations is well covered at the following BBC website: **http://www.bbc.co.uk/history/ancient/romans/pompeii_rediscovery_01.shtml**, while Chapter 2 of *The Complete Pompeii* has a detailed history of the rediscovery of the town. In particular, pages 52–55 contain extensive information about the contribution of Giuseppe Fiorelli to the excavations.

Teaching suggestions

- It is definitely worth reading in class both of the Pliny letters which deal with the eruption – *Letters* 6.16 and 6.20. These are readily available on the internet, or in *Pompeii: a sourcebook*.
- Students who are studying Geography may wish to research the volcanic and tectonic science behind the eruption, as well as the continued threat which Vesuvius presents today.

Houses (Reader, pages 111–114)

To lay the foundations of this topic, it is worthwhile examining with your students the typical layout of a Roman house, and particularly the functions of the atrium, the tablinum and the peristylium, so that they can understand how the House of the Faun and the House of the Vettii differ from this typical model. When studying these houses, it is important to remind your students that they represent the houses of the very wealthy – the vast majority of Pompeians lived in far more humble dwellings.

There are many internet resources for both houses. For the House of the Vettii, the following website gives a detailed room by room description: **http://www.stoa.org/projects/ph/rooms?houseid=18**. A wide variety of photographs can be found at **http://www.pompeiiinpictures.net/R6/6%2015%2001%20plan%202.htm**. For the House of the Faun, there is an excellent 3D reconstruction of the house at the following website: **http://www.capware.it/**. You need to click 'Pompei' on the left and then 'Fauno' on the horizontal menu. There are a good series of photos at **http://www.pompeiiinpictures.net/R6/6%2012%2002%20p1.htm**.

Teaching suggestions

- A good example of a 'typical domus' is the House of the Tragic Poet in Pompeii; the following website has an excellent 'clickable' layout of the house: **http://www.vroma.org/~bmcmanus/house.html**. Once students have studied this, they can then focus on the particular differences of the houses on the specification; these are outlined in the Reader on pages 97–99. Ask students to consider what these individualities might tell us about the owners of each house.
- There is obviously scope to ask students to compare the houses of the Vettii and the Faun with houses today, particularly those of the very wealthy. The more artistic students might want to come up with their own artist's impression of what the houses might have looked like, while there is also great fun to be had from allowing students to imagine that they are 'Roman estate agents' charged with selling the houses – how would they advertise them?

The forum and government
(Reader, pages 108–111)

Both Connolly and Berry have excellent sections in their books on these topics. The website **http://www.capware.it/** has good reconstructions of the forum by choosing 'Pompei' and then 'foro' from the horizontal menu. The following website also has some good information about various buildings of the forum: **http://pompeii.virginia.edu/forummap.html** A good reconstruction of the forum can be viewed at **http://farm4.static.**

flickr.com/3238/3155112933_678b9d4268_o.png.

While teaching this topic, it is a good idea to have students work from their own map of the forum – this could be redesigned from the map in the Reader on page 95. When focusing on the buildings, it might be helpful to divide them into three categories: 'religious', 'commercial' and 'political'. The following list gives some resources for each category:

Religious: The Temple of Jupiter was a centre point of the town and a symbol of Roman power (each Roman town had a similar 'major' temple). Information of inscriptions around the temple can be found on pages 87–89 of *Pompeii: a sourcebook*. The Temple of Apollo is the oldest temple in the forum; pages 84–85 of *Pompeii: a sourcebook* give some background information, while on pages 94–95 of the same book there is some useful material on the Temple of the Emperor. Page 197 of Berry's *The Complete Pompeii* gives helpful information about the possible uses of the Temple of the Public Lares.

Commercial: There is a very good explanation of the Eumachia building on pages 98–99 of *Pompeii: a sourcebook*, while page 179 has some information about the Weights and Measures table. Pages 129–130 of *The Complete Pompeii* gives some information about the Macellum and the Granary. It is well worth getting students to investigate what sort of items were on sale at the markets and what this might tell us about the diet and spending habits of Pompeians.

Political: The political buildings of the forum tie in naturally with the way in which Pompeii was governed. Berry's *The Complete Pompeii* has a good analysis of the civic buildings of the forum on pages 128–130. It should be noted that the name 'basilica' has changed down the ages. It originates from the Greek adjective *basilicos*, meaning 'royal'; in many Greek towns there was a 'royal stoa' in the city centre – an elaborate meeting place where business was conducted. The Romans adapted the word to describe a major public building, often where legal matters were processed; after the Roman empire was Christianised, the word was adapted again to describe the large buildings where people met for worship.

Berry gives a good explanation of the political structure of Pompeii on pages 122–123, while she also has an excellent section on 'politics and propaganda' on pages 131–133. Moreover, chapter 6 of *Pompeii: a sourcebook* is dedicated to evidence of politics in the town and lists all the examples of 'election graffiti'. One of the key points about politics in Pompeii is that people grouped into commercial guilds, much like trade unions today; it was to these groups that political candidates needed to appeal. The Channel 4 documentary *The Private Lives of Pompeii* has a good look at a Pompeian election campaign.

Teaching suggestions

- Ask students to compare modern election campaigns, advertisements and slogans with those of Pompeii.
- Ask students to write an imaginative account of a day in the forum. Perhaps they are a Pompeian who is visiting the forum to go to market, make a sacrifice, or attend a legal case. Encourage them to describe the sights and sounds in as much detail as possible, reflecting on what the buildings and atmosphere of the forum means to them.

Inns and thermopolia

(Reader, pages 115–116)

This is a short topic and relatively easy to cover. There are obvious parallels to make with modern fast food outlets and coffee shops. Berry has some excellent background information on pages 230–233.

The theatre (Reader, pages 118–120)

The Roman theatre was heavily influenced by the Greek theatre, and so it would be worth teachers looking at the material on the latter in the Athens option (see pages 25–30 of the Reader).

Plautus is one of the earliest surviving writers in the canon of Latin literature. He is believed to have lived between 254 and 184 BC and to have been an actor himself. He studied closely the plays of the Greek comic playwright Menander, who was writing in Athens in the late 4th century BC. Most of Plautus' comedies are adapted from Greek models for a Roman audience; in some cases, he has simply rewritten and slightly adapted a Greek play into Latin.

The best book for research on this topic is *The Roman Theatre and its Audience* by R. C. Beacham (Harvard University Press), while detailed information can also be found at **http://homepage.usask.ca/~jrp638/CourseNotes/RomNewCom.html**.

For use with students, Peter Connolly's *The Ancient City* (OUP) has an excellent chapter (pages 182–189) on the Roman theatre, together with a whole series of images and reconstructions, while pages 137–139 of *The Complete Pompeii* has good information about the theatre in Pompeii.

Teaching suggestions

- Students might like to research a play of Plautus, perhaps presenting a synopsis of the plot to the class.
- The more artistic students may enjoy creating artist's impressions of what a Roman theatre might have looked like with a play going on. They could also try to design a typical actor's mask.
- There is scope for some creative writing with students imagining that they are watching a play – they could focus on what they see and hear, both on stage and in the audience.
- Comparisons with the modern theatre are another fertile area; students could be encouraged to draw up a list of similarities and differences between the ancient and modern stage.

The baths (Reader, pages 116–118)

Peter Connolly's *The Ancient City* (pages 238–247) has great detail about Roman baths in general, while pages 62–67 of his *Pompeii* has great detail about the Stabian baths of Pompeii. In addition, pages 150–153 of *The Complete Pompeii* also has excellent information about Pompeii's baths.

One challenge is obviously to get students to learn the names and meanings of the rooms at the baths. Clearly, the *frigidarium* (fridge, frigid) and *tepidarium* (tepid) are words easily associated with English derivations. The *caldarium* is more of a problem since it looks like the English 'cold'. However, it is actually linked to the English word 'scalding' and this is a good way to help students remember that it is the hot room. The *apodyterium* is, regrettably, one which students will just have to learn, while the *palaestra* is also lacking in English derivatives, although students might like to know that it comes from the Greek word *palē*, which meant 'wrestling'.

For some contemporary sources on the baths, the philosopher and statesman Seneca lived next to a bath house in the 1st century AD, and complained about the noise and chaos there in his *Epistle* 56. There is an entertaining (if satirical) description of a visit to the baths in chapters 27 and 28 of Petronius' *Satyricon*.

Teaching suggestions

- The obvious comparison with the modern world is with gyms and sports centres. Unlike the Romans, we do not need to wash at such places because we have washing facilities at home. Students might like to imagine what life is like in a world where most people are not able to wash properly at home!
- If you are within travelling distance of the city of Bath, you might like to organise a trip to the Roman baths there. **http://www.romanbaths.co.uk/** gives plenty of information about the site and is useful for teachers and students even if you are not planning a visit.

The amphitheatre

(Reader, pages 120–121)

Again, this topic is relatively short (if entertaining), since amphitheatres are covered in detail in the Rome option of this specification. There are plenty of resources in the various recommended books on this building, but of particular note is Appendix 1 of *Pompeii: a sourcebook*, which produces a table of all the known games held in the town. The same book gives details of sources linked to the amphitheatre on pages 46ff., while pages 60–63 cover details of the riot in the amphitheatre, including the fresco depicting the event which was found in the House of Actius Anicetus. A good web page with this image and some analysis of the riot is **http://penelope.uchicago.edu/~grout/encyclopaedia_romana/gladiators/pompeii.html**.

Teaching suggestions

- The riot allows you to ask students to make comparisons with violence at sporting events today – football hooliganism being the obvious example.

4 Tackling the Written Examination

Those students who have studied page 122 of the Reader will be familiar with the assessment criteria of knowledge, understanding and interpretation/evaluation (analysis) and will know how to respond to them in their answers. It is useful to draw attention to them whenever examination type work is set.

In many cases the student's level of examination entry, Higher or Foundation, won't be decided until late on in the course. Although the assessment methods are different for each level, the three criteria apply to all students and fortunately the content of the specification lends itself to teaching at both levels. All students need to learn the facts, whether the facts are to be tested by multiple choice or essay. Foundation level students may find essay writing demanding, but can consolidate facts and develop a more critical approach from pre-essay discussion.

Pieces of work can be set with the same subject matter, but with different methods of practice or assessment. For example:

Higher level (Essay)

To what extent was the Great Panathenaia a political as well as religious festival?

Foundation level (Source based question: photograph of Panathenaic frieze)

1. Where was this piece of sculpture and what does it show?
2. What were the main events in the Great Panathenaia?
3. Why was the Great Panathenaia important to Athenian citizens?

Multiple choice questions

These questions are answered only by Foundation level students, but they can be a useful way of testing fact at all levels, particularly if students are feeling insecure.

You might even get certain students to compose multiple choice questions for other members of the class. Having a regular five minute oral multiple choice quiz will get students in the habit of learning facts, if you have a class that responds well to a competitive approach. Doing the test orally, of course, cuts down on the time taken in teacher preparation. If you are doing this kind of exercise, however, it is important to ensure that students concentrate on the most important aspects of a particular topic and don't get carried away setting trick questions on obscure details.

Answers to the multiple choice questions in the Reader:

(page 123) Laps in the Circus Maximus were counted using dolphins (B)

(page 123) The gods

God	Responsibility	Symbol
Example: Neptune	***Sea***	*Trident*
Mercury	Messenger	Winged sandals
Ceres	Fertility	Crops
Vesta	Hearth	Fire

(page 124)
Apollo was a particularly **important** god because he could help people look into the future (B)

(page 124)
The riot in the Amphitheatre in 59 AD was a significant event to Pompeii because:

(i) The emperor banned games for ten years.

(iii) So many Pompeians were killed by their neighbours from Nuceria.

(vi) Many politicians lost the chance to gain the support of the people.

(page 125)
Education of boys and girls in Athens

a) Girls were educated by their fathers. False

b) Girls needed to be educated for a role in politics. False

c) Exercise was an important part of a boy's education. True

d) Learning to weave was an important part of a girl's education. True

e) Boys and girls were taught together. False

(page 126)

A Roman sacrifice

1. worshipper goes to buy an animal
2. dress in ribbons
3. procession
4. pluck lock of hair
5. strike with hammer
6. entrails examined to see if animal healthy

Source-based questions

The format of the source-based questions, which focus in the three questions on fact, understanding and evaluation respectively, provides a good training for the essay question. When you are selecting passages or visuals for questions, choose those which will later be of use in essay questions.

Each source should be chosen to allow candidates, in the three questions, to focus on fact, understanding and evaluation, though not necessarily in that order. Each part of the question, a) b) and c), will cover one AO only. In the majority of cases it will be that a) will test AO1, b) will test AO2 and c) will test AO3. The questions will always follow the most logical order working outwards from the source. For Civilisation (units A351 and A353) this is generally going to be knowledge, then understanding, then evaluation, but not necessarily always. For Literature (A352) the pattern will often go a) AO3, b) AO1 and c) AO2, because they often begin by asking the student to analyse the literary source, then work outwards from there. In the Reader (page 129) you will find a range of questions; it would be useful to encourage students to think about what each is testing.

The sources will be chosen to give the student every opportunity to display knowledge and understanding and their ability to evaluate/interpret the source. They are likely to be chosen from the sorts of books that are recommended in the reading lists. In particular:

- **Athens**: relief and free-standing sculpture, photographs of archaeological remains, ground plans or reconstructions of buildings, artefacts, inscriptions, extracts from literary texts, vase-paintings.
- **Rome**: relief and free-standing sculpture, inscriptions such as tombstones, artefacts, written sources such as Pliny, Juvenal or Martial, photographs, plans or reconstructions of buildings.
- **Homer**: the sources will be passages from the extracts studied.
- **Ovid**: the sources will be passages from the extracts studied.
- **Sparta**: as there is much less material evidence available, the emphasis will be on written sources such as Herodotus, Plutarch, Thucydides, Xenophon, Plato, Aristotle or Pausanias. Students should be aware that the question will not be testing their knowledge of a particular author, but of Sparta. It is worth making sure that students understand the potential bias in some of the authors.
- **Pompeii**: photographs of buildings as they are now, wall-paintings, mosaics and sculpture, reconstructions, drawings, plans, artefacts, Pliny's *Letters*.

Specimen answers to the source-based questions in the Reader

(page 127)

(a) How is this theatre typical of a Roman theatre?

This question requires students to identify key features of the theatre that you would find in others. This is interpretation of the source (AO3).

The theatre is open-air. There is a high ornate backdrop which looks as though it had niches and perhaps statues in it. The lower area of the backdrop suggests three doorways/openings which is typical of a street scene in Roman comedy. The stage is raised above the semi-circular area and there is a space at the foot of it for a curtain.

In front of the stage is a semicircular or D shaped area where seats would be put for important people, and musicians would sometimes play. There is an arched entrance beside the stage used by VIPs, and above the arch, seating for the sponsor.

The seats are arranged in a three-quarter circle in tiers, which are divided into levels for different members of the community.

Above the arched entrance near the stage is a place where the guest of honour could sit to watch the play.

(b) Explain how comfortable a Roman audience was when watching a play.

This question requires students to show their factual knowledge of the theatre and aspects of comfort (AO1). In choosing what they refer to here students have to consider relevant facts.

The theatre was open air so the audience may have got too hot in summer. However, there was a canopy to keep off the sun, and sometimes water or perfume was sprinkled to make the audience feel more comfortable.

The seats were made of stone, and the plays could last all day, so this was uncomfortable for them. There was no division between seats, and people in the audience must have been squashed together. People could take cushions with them to be more comfortable.

Those sitting in the orchestra at the front would have been more comfortable because there was more space and they had special seats.

(c) Explain why Roman comedies were entertaining for a lower class Roman audience.

This question tests students' understanding of Roman comedies (AO2).

The audience had a clear all-round view and good acoustics meant that even from the top tiers they could enjoy what was happening on stage. They could appreciate the masks and recognise the stock characters. The type of humour, which was fairly crude, with slapstick, rude jokes and sexual gestures would have been very entertaining to them. The stories were easy to understand: they often had stock characters such as the young lovesick son, bad-tempered father and cheeky slave, such as can be found in the plays of Plautus. What appealed particularly to the lower class audience was the way in which the master of the household, i.e. a higher class citizen, was made to look stupid by those around him – quite often the slave. There were times in the play when the actors called directly to the audience, and invited them to mock the characters. This would have been very entertaining. Finally, the fact that it was a holiday, and they were all sitting close together and able to share the jokes, must have made the theatre an entertaining place.

(page 128)

(a) Describe how and why the Spartans took over the helots' land.

This question asks students to show their factual knowledge of Spartan history (AO1).

The Dorian invaders who settled in Sparta in Laconia wanted to control the native inhabitants of Laconia, the Achaean Greeks. They captured them and forced them to work as serfs on Spartan farms. They were called helots, or captives. A war broke out between the Spartans and the Messenians, their neighbours on the west, which, after a struggle with Messenia lasting for twenty years, ended in the capture of the Messenians, who were forced to pay half the produce of the soil as tribute to their Spartan overlords.

The Spartans did this so that they would have no opposition to their rule; they took over fertile land on which they could produce, through the helots, plenty of food for themselves. This left them free to develop their militaristic society.

(b) Explain how and why the Spartans treated the helots badly.

This question tests students' understanding of what motivated the Spartans to behave the way they did (AO2).

The helots had no political rights. At the beginning of every year the Spartans declared war on them, which meant that it was legal to kill them. They hunted them, and the *Krypteia* executed any helots who might pose a danger. Some were publicly beaten to ensure the submission of the rest. The helots were forced to do degrading things – they were deliberately made to get drunk and look foolish so that Spartan children would be warned off drink. Helots were not trained but sometimes had to fight.

The helots outnumbered the Spartans by at least 10:1 and could therefore have overcome the Spartan masters if they had had the freedom to get together and plot. They were harshly treated to prevent them from having the opportunity to get together. Keeping the helots submissive and doing the work of farmers and slaves was important because it gave the Spartans the time to do what they wanted ie fight.

(c) Can the Spartans' treatment of this class of society be justified? Explain your opinions.

This question asks students to make judgements about Sparta in the context of their society; this is a form of evaluation (AO3).

From our point of view, this treatment cannot be justified. The helots had to work hard on the land, but were forced to hand over half of what they produced. They were put to death by the *Krypteia* without having committed any crime, and without a trial. They were humiliated, by being made to get drunk, wear a dog-skin cap, just to act as bad examples to young Spartans. They were sent out to fight for Sparta even though they had had no training, and they were actually declared enemies of Sparta. All this goes against human rights and is completely unjustifiable.

The Spartans would justify their treatment by saying that the helots were lucky to have a farm and be allowed to keep surplus produce; they could live with their families, and were allowed religious freedom. Their treatment could be justified by the fact that they were an essential part of the structure of Spartan society: whilst they did the farming, the perioikoi could engage in trade and produce crafts and the Spartiates could take part in the government, and, most important, devote themselves to fighting. The Greeks did not believe that slavery in itself was wrong, and so the Spartans did not see their behaviour as immoral.

Essay questions

The Reader gives students guidance on how to check that the assessment criteria have been met.

The specification lists aspects of each option which are for particular study. The examination questions might cut across several aspects, but to begin with, set essay titles which relate to a specific one. If you prepare essays under the aspect headings, you will then have a checklist and know that students have had the opportunity to write on the range of aspects. As you give out the titles, discuss what strengths you need to answer a particular question. When it comes to the examination, students will have to make an informed decision about what they can score most highly on.

These are the kind of essay titles that relate to aspects of study in the Epic and Myth unit:

Homer, The Odyssey

- *Odysseus as hero* – Does Odysseus always appear heroic in the books you have read?

- *Characters* – The Odyssey is enjoyable because Homer depicts human nature so well. What evidence have you found in the books you have read to support this statement?
- *The gods* – Do you think the gods and goddesses make the *Odyssey* more or less exciting?
- *Women* – Are the women in the *Odyssey* more of a help or hindrance to Odysseus?
- *Xenia* – To what extent is *xenia* important in the books of the *Odyssey* that you have read?
- *Narrative technique* – What makes Homer such a good storyteller?

Ovid, Metamorphoses

- *Characters* – Which female characters do you find most convincing? (Discuss at least four.)
- *Morality* – Does Ovid aim to give us a moral lesson, or are his stories mainly for entertainment?
- *The gods* – Is it true to say that the behaviour of the gods is much worse than that of the humans who suffer?
- *Emotions and relationships* – 'Ovid shows great skill in portraying relationships between husbands and wives and parents and children'. What evidence do you have of this in your reading of the *Metamorphoses*?
- *Ovid's narrative and descriptive technique* – What makes Ovid such a good storyteller?

For the Epic and Myth unit, where characters are not named in the specification there will not be essay questions set specifically on them, though they might well be used as evidence in other essays. They could, however, be the subject of a source-based question.

When setting essays, introduce one challenge at a time. For the first essay you might give no restrictions at all on its production. The next might have to be written within a time limit, but be done with prepared notes; the next might have to be done under examination conditions.

Give students a copy of the Assessment Grid. It will help them to see where they need to put their efforts in order to pick up more marks. They could even be invited to mark their own essays and justify the marks they have given.

Sample essay responses

Handouts 1 and 2 (pages 72–75) provide two examination-type answers to the following essay question: 'Is the moral of the *Metamorphoses* simply that bad behaviour is always punished?' They are followed by examiner comments in the light of the Higher Tier Section B Assessment Grid.

Handouts 3 and 4 (pages 76–79) provide two examination-type answers to the following essay question: 'Explain to what extent theatre was an important part of Athenian life.' They are followed by examiner comments in the light of the Higher Tier Section B Assessment Grid.

5 Culture and Society in the Classical World: the Controlled Assessment (Unit A354)

Introduction

The controlled assessment is the internally assessed unit. Each year on 1 June OCR publishes two essay titles for each of the six options, one of which is to be completed before the following May. There is a word limit of 2000 words. It is the teacher's job to give the student a grounding in the relevant subject; give out the title, support the student during the research phase, supervise the writing up under controlled conditions and finally to mark the essay. For further details, see the specification, sections 4–5.

Choosing an option

Given that the controlled assessment needs considerable teacher input, the choice of option has to be the teacher's. There is no obligation to choose the same option for all students, but it makes it much more manageable to do so, as the teacher has to provide the underpinning knowledge and resources and oversee the research process.

In making your decision you will need to bear in mind:

- The resources you have available.
- Your personal knowledge and strengths
- The interests and abilities of your students
- The options you have chosen elsewhere on the paper. For example, if you have chosen Athens in your City Life unit, you will have more context for *Lysistrata* or *Antigone* than if you have chosen Rome. Those who have chosen Rome and Pompeii will have underpinning knowledge for Pliny's *Letters* or the *Aeneid*.
- Your school or college environment. Your geographical location may mean that Romano-British evidence is on your doorstep; you may have a Drama department keen to put on *Antigone*; a strong sporting ethos may make the Olympic Games an obvious choice.

Key skills

Students will need to develop the following skills in preparing for and writing their essay:

- understanding the content of the source material
- understanding the social and cultural context
- assessing the usefulness of the source(s) as evidence
- conducting independent research
- constructing an essay.

Content. Less able students may require support with the basic comprehension of texts or help with archaeological terminology, for example, before they can move on to evaluating the material or engaging in research. Giving them a manageable section of the text to read, together with some basic comprehension questions, might give them confidence in following a narrative account; a glossary of terms, a chronology and a list of key names might enable them to make more sense of an archaeological report.

Social and cultural context. It is the teacher's job to ensure that the student has a good enough grounding in the context to enable him or her to make sense of, and reasoned judgements about, the evidence. For example, a student could not appreciate the themes to be studied in the *Lysistrata* option without knowing something about the Peloponnesian war, the role of women, or the nature of Greek theatre. The background knowledge will not be tested *per se*, but without it the student is unlikely to demonstrate understanding of the source (AO2), or the ability to interpret, evaluate, or respond to it (AO3). The information and questions in the Reader aim to help the student develop an awareness of the context as well as the themes.

The source as evidence. Guidance on how to assess primary source material is crucial if the student is to meet the assessment criteria. The main points to get across are:

- relevance: do the chronology and location match the evidence needed?
- reliability: is there doubt about identification or meaning in the eyes of scholars?
- context: is it by nature biased?
- appropriateness: is it applicable to the question being researched?

The student will need to be reminded that *Antigone*, for example, cannot be taken as evidence for the behaviour of real people in 5th-century Athens, or that a vase-painting of an Olympic event may include some artistic licence. Pages 172–173 in the Reader give guidance about interpreting evidence.

Independent research. Students will need guidance in the effective use of their research time. Careful preparation of booklists, materials and website advice are also needed to prevent them from downloading pages of irrelevant material which they don't understand.

Constructing an essay. The process of writing an essay of 2000 words which responds to assessment criteria needs practice. One way to do this is to take a different essay question and work through an essay plan as a group, looking at how to write an introduction which establishes what issues are raised by the title; order paragraphs to ensure that the argument flows; state the argument and use primary evidence to support it in each paragraph; arrive at a logical conclusion.

Planning your teaching

The controlled assessment is compulsory for both the full and short course GCSE; it is worth 25% and 50% of the marks respectively. Clearly, it is an integral part of the course, not an add-on. Plan to spend a proportionate amount of your time on preparing your candidates for it. Although you may have the controlled assessment essay titles in front of you, don't focus on them from the beginning, any more than you would begin teaching any option with one particular examination question in mind. As the specification states: 'Candidates will have to take part in a planned learning programme that covers the underpinning knowledge and skills of the unit in addition to completing the evidence requirements of the designated assessment tasks.'

The specification anticipates fifteen hours for individual research and five hours for writing up under controlled conditions. Use the rest of the time you have available for preparing your students as you would for any other examination topic.

Considering the following questions will help you plan:

- When will you start on the underpinning knowledge, bearing in mind the other units you are teaching?
- At what point will you issue the titles and establish which one your students are to work towards. Will you allow them to choose either of the two questions on offer, or will you select the title?
- Where will the students do their research? Might you need to book an IT room for some of their lesson time?
- When will you schedule your controlled assessment? Will it be your choice or will you have to fit into an all-school scheme? Do you need to avoid clashes with other subjects? Can you manage the assessment within your timetabled slots?

Choosing your source material

Specific themes are listed in the specification in order to help reduce the evidence to something which is manageable both in its quantity and level of difficulty at GCSE standard. Clearly, where a play is set the whole of the play has to be read, but the teacher can select which of Pliny's letters to read, which parts of the *Aeneid*, or which towns and villas to study.

Once the student has been given the essay title, you may advise on research material. The controlled assessment essay titles will obviously have a bearing on what evidence the teacher makes available. The specification states: 'Candidates can approach the questions in a number of different ways and in varying levels of depth, meaning that with guidance from teachers tasks can be adapted to suit centre and candidate specific circumstances.' This means that, although you cannot change the wording of the title, you can, by judicious advice, make sure that each student is performing at an appropriate level.

One of the specimen questions for the Virgil option, for example, is: 'Is the plot of the *Aeneid* driven more by gods or by human characters?' Clearly there is scope here to use the whole of the *Aeneid* and, indeed, there will be very able students who can deal with the amount of material that would be involved in researching all twelve books.

However, most students will require assistance as to where to look for evidence of the gods directing events. The Virgil section below sets out the books which are rich in evidence for all the themes (Books 1, 2, 4, 6, 12) and adds a few more specific references from other books. The average student can probably work with this volume of material, find the relevant evidence for the gods' actions and collect a good body of data for the controlled assessment.

You may feel that for some students five books would represent an overwhelming volume of material. In that case it would be in order for the student to be given just one or two books for research, or just specific passages to study.

Suggestions for sources relating to each option, including secondary reading, are given in the relevant sections of this chapter below. Sometimes it may be appropriate for students to use in their analysis and evaluation primary sources additional to the main literary text. For example, in assessing Pliny's relationship with his household they may draw upon evidence from other writers such as Martial or Juvenal; in discussing the staging of *Antigone* archaeological evidence may be an important element in their argument.

Preparing your resources

The main source for the literary topics will be the text; for the others you will need a comprehensive source-based text book or resources you have assembled yourself.

There is a vast amount of material available on the classical world, and keen students can often reproduce far too much secondary reading or copy down primary source material indiscriminately. You can help by drawing up a list of other relevant resources and issuing it to the students. This might include library books, website addresses and materials held in the classroom for consultation during lessons. Another advantage of issuing a list is that it helps students to compile their bibliography. Ideas on useful resources are given in later sections of this chapter. Bear in mind that finding sources and deciding which ones to use is part of the research process, so you should offer guidance only where appropriate.

Some students may benefit from having a copy of the marking criteria. For others, using the assessment criteria as a sort of checklist can help maintain a more disciplined approach:

- AO1 Does the evidence I have written down directly help me to answer the question? Am I sure that my facts are accurate? Am I using primary evidence or repeating what someone else has written?
- AO2 Can I explain fully why I think that the evidence proves my point?
- AO3 Am I answering the question?

Don't allow yourself to be faced with the student who, on controlled assessment day, pathetically announces that the research is on a computer which has just crashed, in a file that has gone missing, in a format that can't be read ...! Arm yourself with some pocket files, one for each student, and insist that a hard copy of all research be placed in it after every lesson or once a week.

That way, the student will always have research to work with, and you will have the reassurance of evidence of work in progress.

Ensure that your students have any materials that will help them in the research process, such as: a copy of the question, with a reminder that the wording of the question cannot be changed; the facility to photocopy evidence; a way of showing what evidence they want to use, such as highlighter pens; a file in which to keep papers; a USB to make an electronic back-up of material and transport it between home and school (don't let them rely on email); a copy of the assessment criteria or a checklist which helps them to respond to the criteria; a pro forma which helps them to compile their bibliography.

Marking

For teachers who have never done coursework, the responsibility of marking may weigh heavily. The secret is not to think about marks, but to find the statement in the marking criteria grid that best describes the essay and then award the corresponding mark.

Discuss assessment with your colleagues. If you are working alone, find someone in another school or college with whom you can share ideas. Follow the instructions issued by OCR and take the opportunity to attend INSET meetings.

Sophocles, Antigone

Themes

- role and characterisation of Antigone and Creon
- the role and characterisation of the other characters and the Chorus
- the role of women
- the role of the gods, oracles, and fate
- Sophocles' literary and dramatic techniques and the staging of the play

Contexts

- Greek mythological background
- the performance of the play and its audience
- the literary and cultural context of the play
- the political, social and moral context of the play
- the continuing influence of Sophoclean drama on later times, and similarities and differences between the ideas and values expressed in Sophocles' *Antigone* and those of later times

Specimen essay titles

EITHER

- How would an ancient Athenian audience have responded to Antigone's behaviour in Sophocles' *Antigone*?

OR

- How do Antigone and Ismene differ in their views on the role of women in society?

Why choose this option?

Students who have studied Athens will already know about how citizens had to contribute to the running of the state through attending the assembly and participating in the law courts. They will also have an understanding of how the play might have been received at its first performance. Those who have studied Sparta, too, will have developed an awareness of the individual and state and will be well prepared for some of the issues raised by Sophocles. However, the main focus of the unit is on the text itself as evidence, and the Athens chapter of the Reader provides those who have studied the Roman topics with a sound view of the social and cultural context of the play.

Close reading of the text is essential for this option, and those who get on well with English literature are likely to do well. The play itself is quite short (1,500 lines), and so not too daunting for those who would struggle with a longer text. The actual body of material they have to deal with in their research is clearly defined and contained, a certain advantage for those with limited facilities for broad research or who would find it difficult to manage the collection and organisation of material from disparate sources. The issues, of course, involve abstract thought, but at this level can be reduced to points which are within the grasp and experience of the student. The Reader puts the students on the right track for each aspect designated in the specification, and poses questions to get them relating the play to their own experiences. The aspect of teenage rebellion and the intransigence of authority could well be the thing that makes this option attractive for certain groups.

Key resources

The translation by Fagles, *Sophocles: The Three Theban Plays* (Penguin) is readily available, contains the Oedipus plays for any students who might want to extend their knowledge, has a sound introduction and benefits from having an excellent companion: *Sophocles Antigone and Oedipus the King: A Companion to the Penguin Translation* by John Wilkins and Matthew Macleod (Bristol Classical Press/Duckworth). As well as the commentary, the companion has background and useful summaries on myth, characters, themes and technique. Teachers might also use the D. Franklin translation (CUP).

Good resources for the teacher are Oliver Taplin, *Greek Tragedy in Action* (Routledge) and David Wiles, *Greek Theatre Performance* (CUP), which focus on performance. David Carter's *The Politics of Greek Tragedy* (Bristol Phoenix Press) makes excellent reading on the political context; on Sophocles there is D. Winnington-Ingram, *Sophocles: an Interpretation* (CUP). For the context of 5th-century Athens, James Renshaw, *In Search of the Greeks* (Bristol Classical Press) and *JACT World of Athens* (CUP) provide excellent material.

For the student, *The Greek and Roman Stage* by David Taylor (Bristol Classical Press) gives a clear introduction to the Greek theatre specifically for GCSE level pupils, and has the added advantage that it takes *Antigone* as a major example, working out how three actors managed to play all the roles. Marion Baldock's *Greek Tragedy: An Introduction* (Bristol Classical Press) is designed for A Level, but there is much in it to guide the able GCSE student or support the teacher. *Antigone; Oedipus the King; Electra* translated by Kitto is useful for the commentary by Edith Hall (OUP) where she relates the translation to Greek concepts and shades of meaning: access to it would benefit some students.

Teaching suggestions

- *Antigone* has a simple plot and easily comprehensible characters, and it should not be difficult to get a class involved in the story and reacting to the people in it.
- A good way to introduce students to the play is through a production. The video of the 1984 BBC version with Juliet Stevenson is ideal. Unfortunately it is not available commercially, but there are at least clips on YouTube. If no production is available, a class reading is a good introduction.
- The first watching/reading can focus on Antigone and Creon. After each scene, the class can assess how much sympathy they feel for Antigone/Creon and why. A gimmick such as a 'swingometer' with individuals invited to move the needle according to the class consensus about the characters encourages participation. The activity is accessible at all levels and promotes an analytical approach. The reasons they put forward for their reactions – the character is arrogant, an insecure leader, attention-seeking, a rebel, too hardhearted, can't stand being challenged by a woman, unrealistic, has had a difficult family background, brought it on herself – may be spontaneous responses but will introduce them to aspects of the play that they have to study formally.

Aristophanes, Lysistrata

Themes

- the role and characterisation of Lysistrata
- the role and characterisation of the other characters and the Chorus
- the role of women
- Aristophanes' dramatic and literary techniques
- contemporary events referred to in the play

Contexts

- the historical context of the play
- the political, social and cultural context of the play
- the performance of the play and its audience
- the continuing influence of Aristophanic comedy on later times, and similarities and differences between the ideas and values expressed in Aristophanes' *Lysistrata* and those of later times

Specimen essay titles

EITHER

- How successful was Aristophanes in making the *Lysistrata* amusing for his audience?

OR

- How would you adapt Aristophanes' *Lysistrata* for a modern day audience?

Why choose this option?

Students who have studied Athens will be aware of the democracy. They will also have an understanding of how the play might have been received at its first performance. Those who have studied Sparta, too, will have had an introduction to Spartan women and know something about the Peloponnesian war, and so will be well prepared for some of the issues raised by Aristophanes. However, the main focus of the unit is on the text itself as evidence, and the Athens chapter of the Reader provides those who have studied the Roman topics with a sound view of the social and cultural context of the play.

You will need to consider the acceptability of the subject matter in the school – check with your head teacher if you think the prominence of the erect phallus could cause offence! You will know whether your class would warm to the subject matter and humour of the play, and it could be that what would be a great hit one year would be an embarrassing flop the next.

The main focus of the research is on the content of the play, which is not long (1,300 lines) – an advantage for those who find reading long texts daunting.

Key resources

The translation by Sommerstein in *Lysistrata and Other Plays* (Penguin) is readable and conveys the comedy well. Students can use the notes, but will probably need help from the teacher in understanding some of the terms used in them. *The Archarnians* is in the same volume. Some students might like to read this play, as it also deals with an attempt to end the Peloponnesian war.

For the teacher, Douglas MacDowell, *Aristophanes and Athens* (OUP) is worth buying. It deals with intention and interpretation, the Athenian context and the audience and its expectations, as well as having a whole chapter on *Lysistrata*. E. Bowie also includes a chapter just on *Lysistrata* in *Aristophanes: myth, ritual and comedy* (CUP). Paul Cartledge, *Aristophanes and the Theatre of the Absurd* (Bristol Classical Press) is a full and informative introduction, written with A level students in mind but useful for teachers and accessible to the more able GCSE students.

Pamela Bradley, *Ancient Greece: using evidence* (CUP) gives a very clear account of Greece and Sparta, useful for quick reference as well as more detailed study. If you want a primary source on the war, read Thucydides, *The Peloponnesian War* (translation by R. Warner, Penguin). Other useful reading about Aristophanes includes K. J. Dover,

Aristophanic Comedy (California) and P. Easterling and Knox, *Greek Drama* (CUP).

For students, David Taylor, *The Greek and Roman Stage* is well-illustrated with primary source material, as is Robin Barrow, *Athenian Democracy* (both Bristol Classical Press). The latter provides a clear and comprehensive account of democracy, including a chapter on the Peloponnesian war, with plenty of subheadings which will help students focus their research. The text points out continually the difficulties of interpreting source material. The Lysistrata Game on **www.classicspage.com** is an amusing way for students to check their knowledge of the plot. Peter Connolly's *The Ancient City* (OUP) includes reconstructions of Athens which will allow students to picture the places mentioned in the play.

Teaching suggestions

- There is so much involved in appreciating a play by Aristophanes – the nature of Greek theatre, the comic process and historical context – that to be launched into it without a grounding in at least one of these strands could lead to a dispiriting experience for the student. One way to introduce the play, therefore, is to watch a favourite comedy together in class.
- Any formal analysis of comedy will probably be new to students, but in discussing why they find their favourite film or TV programme funny they can begin the analysis on familiar territory. Class discussion will bring up farce, fantasy, situation, satire, sexual innuendo, scatological jokes, inappropriate behaviour and stereotypes. They should then be ready to apply their own criteria to *Lysistrata*.

The Olympic Games

Candidates will be expected to demonstrate a detailed knowledge of relevant archaeological and literary evidence.

Themes

- organisation of the Olympic Games
- programme of events
- preparation for and participation in the Games
- competitors and officials
- religious aspects of the Games
- the site of Olympia

Contexts

- the origins of the Games
- the cultural and political significance of the Games
- spectators and their experiences of the Games
- the continuing influence of the Olympic Games on later times, and similarities and differences between the ancient Olympic Games and the Olympic Games of today

Specimen essay titles

EITHER

- To what extent was warfare a major contributor to the events of the ancient Olympic Games?

OR

- To what extent are the values of the modern Olympic Games based on the values of the ancient Olympic Games?

Why choose this option?

This option is in some ways a very individual one – it relates to the entire Greek world rather than one city, and focuses primarily on sport. However, there are various overlaps with other options. First of all, the Games lasted into the centuries of Roman rule in the Greek world, and they became as important to the Romans as they were to the Greeks. Secondly, there are clear overlaps with the sporting events at the Panathenaic Games in the Athens option, while Roman chariot racing evolved from the equivalent practised in the Greek world, most famously at Olympia. Religion is also at the heart of the ancient Olympics: it is important to know about the role of Zeus as father of the gods (studied in the Athens option, or as 'Jupiter' in the Rome option) in order to understand the religious nature of the games.

Clearly, students with a keen interest in sport will love this topic. It gives them an opportunity to research how ancient competitors trained and performed. In many sports, such as boxing, horse-riding and running, there is the chance to compare how these events differ in their ancient and modern forms. However, this topic is not just about sporting events. There is the possibility of researching the foundation myths of the games, and reflecting on what these stories might tell us about how the games evolved; students who are interested in the interpretation of myth will enjoy this. In addition, students interested in the design of temples and other religious buildings will have the chance to find out about the many religious buildings at the heart of the site in Olympia.

Key resources

There are plenty of good resources here. For a teacher, Nigel Spivey's *The Ancient Olympics* (OUP) offers a detailed but readable overview from an academic's perspective. Similar, but older, is Finlay and Pleket's *The Olympic Games* (Viking Press). A book which will help both teachers and students is Judith Swaddling's *The Ancient Olympic Games* (British Museum Press), while chapter 2 of James Renshaw's *In Search of the Greeks* (Duckworth) gives a comprehensive overview of the games for this specification.

In addition, there are plenty of good resources on the internet. The official site of the IOC has a detailed section on the ancient games, and also allows students to research modern events too: **http://www.olympic.org/uk/games/ancient/index_uk.asp**. Sydney's Powerhouse Museum produced a superb site to coincide with the 2000 games: **http://www.powerhousemuseum.com/greek/**, which contains some excellent reconstructions. **www.insearchofthegreeks.com** has many links as well as a large gallery of photos from Olympia. Another comprehensive site is provided by the Perseus website: **http://www.perseus.tufts.edu/Olympics/**.

Teachers and students who want to do specific research on Pausanias could invest in a translation of his *Guide to Greece* – the relevant books are 5 and 6. However, this is a very detailed guide and there is a lot of material to get through about Olympia, much of it barely relevant to GCSE level. Teachers may wish instead to browse through this very good e-text version, listed here to begin where Pausanias arrives at Olympia: **http://www.theoi.com/Text/Pausanias5A.html#5**.

Teaching suggestions

- This topic gives students great scope to imagine themselves to be characters at the ancient games. Encourage your students to write a diary, a newspaper report, or a letter home; they could imagine they were athletes, spectators, judges, or trainers. They should think about the whole atmosphere of the games and the site of Olympia as well as the events themselves.
- A similar exercise would be to get them to imagine that they are ancient tour guides at Olympia (who actually did exist) and to describe how they would conduct a tour. All these exercises have the advantage of challenging them to get under the skin of all those who attended the games.
- To help students get to grips with all the events, you could ask them to draw up a list with the rules for each event, as well as examining famous athletes. They might research Alkibiades or Kyniska (chariot racing), Leonidas of Rhodes (running), Diagoras of Rhodes (boxing), Milo of Croton (wrestling), Theagenes of Thasos (pankration). Sadly, the horse-riding and pentathlon events haven't left us with any great heroic figures.
- Another obvious way to develop the topic is to ask students to compare the events at the ancient and modern games. This applies to all the major events apart from chariot racing.
- To encourage them to get to know the programme for the festival, ask them to design a 'match programme' such as are on sale at sporting events today.
- A further point of comparison is the rewards due to victors in the ancient and modern games. There is an obvious overlap in that in both eras athletes could expect to benefit much more from endorsements when they return home than when actually at the games.

Virgil, The Aeneid

Themes

- Aeneas' mission
- characterisation of Aeneas and other main characters
- the role of the hero
- the role of the gods and fate
- Virgil's literary techniques

Contexts

- historical context in which the epic was written
- Virgil and his relationship with the Augustan regime
- social, moral and cultural context of the epic
- the continuing influence of Virgil's *Aeneid* on later times, and similarities and differences between the ideas and values expressed in *The Aeneid* and those of later times

Candidates are not required to demonstrate knowledge of the whole text; and when completing the Controlled Assessment task can choose which relevant sections to refer to.

Specimen questions

EITHER

- To what extent is *The Aeneid* more about a nation than an individual?

OR

- Is the plot of *The Aeneid* driven more by gods or by human characters?

Why choose this option?

Those who have studied Rome will have an idea of the political and social context, and *Odyssey* readers will already know what to expect from an epic. However, much is to be gained from studying the *Aeneid* whatever other options have been studied. It encompasses Roman values and religion, mythology, complex characterisation and political propaganda as well as being an exciting story.

The story is likely to have wide appeal: some will go for the gory bits, and others will be drawn into the affair with Dido or the visit to the underworld. The students who do well in this option will be those who enjoy close reading of the text, and who are prepared to look beyond the story to the deeper meanings.

Key resources

Which translation? *Selections from the Aeneid* by Graham Tingay (CUP) uses well-chosen extracts to tell the story, and is less daunting than a full translation. The Penguin translation by David West is clear and accessible, and using the full version gives the more adventurous students greater scope for wider research.

The themes of Aeneas as hero, his character and his mission are interrelated; students will find plenty of evidence for these themes in Books 1, 2, 4, 6 and 12. In addition the description of his shield (Book 8 lines 581–731) provides good evidence for his heroic status as well as for links with Augustus, and Book 10 lines 426–605 tells of the death of Pallas and Aeneas' reaction to it.

The same books provide ample evidence for the gods and fate. It may also be useful to look at Allecto, the Fury sent by Juno (Book 7 lines 286–571), and the representations Venus and Juno make to Jupiter in Book 10 lines 1–117.

Of the main characters apart from Aeneas, Dido appears in Books 1 and 4, and briefly in lines 440–476 of Book 6; Amata is poisoned by Allecto in Book 7 (see above), and briefly appears in Book 12; we see Latinus in Book 7 lines 37–285, and when he tries to dissuade Turnus from fighting at the beginning of Book 12; Turnus can be researched in Book 7 lines 406–474 and throughout Book 12; Aeneas' father, Anchises, appears in Book 2, as do his son, Ascanius/Iulus, and wife, Creusa. They are significant because his family is so important to Aeneas.

Evidence of Virgil's narrative technique can be found throughout, but Books 2, 4 and 6 provide ample material.

The Aeneid of Virgil: A commentary based on the translation of Day Lewis (Bristol Classical Press) by R. D. Williams contains an introduction of use to all students, clear summaries of the books and a commentary and glossary which function well for any translation. Richard Jenkyns, *Classical Epic: Homer and Virgil* (Bristol Classical Press) would make stimulating reading for the more able student.

For the teacher, *Aeneas and the Roman Hero* by R. Deryck Williams (Bristol Classical Press), *Virgil: The Aeneid* by K. W. Gransden (CUP) and W. Camps, *An Introduction to Virgil's Aeneid* (OUP) all provide relevant background information and analysis of the text. These books are also accessible to the more able students.

The notes in Latin editions of the text can be invaluable for exploring references in the text. **http://www.vergil.org/** has very good links to specialised aspects of Virgil. For easy reference to the text, use the online translation at **www.tonykline.co.uk/PITBR/Latin/Virgilhome.htm** which gives detailed summaries of each book together with precise line references.

For further information on the historical background, Pamela Bradley, *Using the Evidence: Ancient Rome* (CUP) provides useful information, much of it in a helpful schematic form. David Shotter, *Augustus Caesar* (Routledge) and Andrew Wallace Hadrill, *Augustan Rome* (Bristol Classical Press) give clear accounts of the period. There are several primary sources that complement the *Aeneid*: the *res gestae* or *Deeds of the Divine Augustus* is Augustus' own account of his achievements, and Suetonius' *Lives of the Twelve Caesars* includes a less idealistic picture of the Emperor (both available online at **www.fordham.edu/halsall/ancient/asbook09.html**).

Teaching suggestions

- Listening to a recording can be very effective. The Naxos dramatised abridged audio CD of the C. Day Lewis translation is accessible, and has the bonus of reminding students that the poetry was composed to be listened to, not read. If your timetable allows, a serialised playing of the suggested books, with pauses at cliff-hangers, can give students time to absorb the story, provides regular opportunities for recapping and can create a genuine sense of anticipation.
- The time students need to take in the basic chronology, geography, characters and relationships should not be underestimated. These things have to be firmly established before any of the underlying themes and ideas – the mission, fate, subtleties of character – can be discussed, let alone researched independently.
- The students will be aware from the Reader of the main thrust of each theme given in the specification. To develop a critical approach, choose an extract which clearly relates to one or more of the themes, is within the students' experience and is likely to cause some genuine argument. Aeneas' leaving Dido in Book 4 can usually be relied upon to engage students' interest and lead them to look at character, the demands of duty, the nature of heroism and the role of fate and the gods; it also introduces them to some very powerful use of language.

Pliny, Letters

Themes

- his character as shown in the letters
- his purpose in writing and publishing the letters
- his relationship with and attitudes to his family and household
- his relationship with Trajan
- his role as a provincial governor

Contexts

- Pliny's life and career
- the social, political and cultural context of his letters
- his intended audience

Candidates are not expected to have a detailed knowledge of all Pliny's Letters; and when completing the Controlled Assessment task can choose which relevant Letters to refer to.

Specimen questions

EITHER

- Pliny says, 'Slaves always have two sides to their nature. They act with reason like men. They also act by instinct like animals.' Do you think that this is an accurate reflection of Pliny's attitude to slaves?

OR

- To what extent is Pliny 'a man who thinks a great deal of others, but even more of himself'?

Why choose this option?

This option complements the Rome and Pompeii options, introducing students to a famous inhabitant of Rome and visitor to the Bay of Naples. However, those who have studied the Greek options can successfully use Pliny as a means to learn about daily life in Rome, backed up by the relevant chapters in the Reader.

The nature of the material means that it is well suited to students for whom shorter pieces are preferable to long narratives. It also appeals to those who are drawn towards life and customs rather than literature *per se*. Of course they will have to take into account the purpose of the letters, their reliability as evidence and the finer points of Pliny's expression, but they will have plenty of opportunity to learn more about slavery, family life, houses, marriage, work and leisure

Key resources

The translation by Greig in *Pliny: A selection of his letters* (CUP) is designed for the GCSE student and has the letters divided into sections: Familia; Public Life; Pliny as a Businessman; Pliny as a Writer and Bithynia. Each section has an introduction which gives the student essential background information. The Reader takes its headings from the themes listed in the specification, and includes references to letters which are not in Greig. You may want to use Greig as the main book, and have copies of the Penguin translation by Betty Radice available for further research. The essay title will determine which letters you need to use.

There are very few critical works on Pliny, but the real need here is not for literary criticism anyway: it is for the teacher to be able to provide context material for the themes which have to be studied. Sourcebooks such as Jo-Ann Shelton, *As the Romans Did* (OUP) and Suzanne Dixon, *The Roman Family* (Johns Hopkins University Press) contain useful material, but students will need reminders about the relevant period and location of the evidence. Horace, Martial, Juvenal and Petronius are all mentioned in the Reader. The Penguin editions provide accessible translations, but you may want to exercise some censorship with regard to which bits to allow students to read.

Students may benefit from reading *Roman Provincial Administration* by John Richardson, *Slavery in Ancient Rome* by M. Massey and P. Mooreland, *Roman Society* by David Taylor and *Penelope to Poppaea* by Anne Haward (all Bristol

Classical Press), as they provide relevant material at the right level. The Cambridge Latin Course website **www.cambridgescp.com** is extremely useful. Stage 37, for example, provides details of the *cursus honorum*, and links lead to much useful detail about Pliny and the background to his letters.

Teaching suggestions

- The aim is to get the students involved with the character of Pliny. The Reader groups the letters under the themes from the specification: taking the letters from one of these themes would make a coherent way to begin. One of the best ways to get students to react to Pliny is to select letters where his character comes over strongly. Few students will be able to restrain their reactions when hearing what he has to say about Calpurnia's love and admiration for him, for example.
- Students often find the concept of writing letters for publication a difficult one. Getting them to think about what people do today to publish their ideas – letters to newspapers, blogs, autobiographies, radio and television appearances as well as collections of correspondence – can be a good place to start. They will then, perhaps, talk about the reasons for publication and think about issues of bias and concern with reputation. Pliny and patronage may feel like an alien topic at first, but being in with the 'right set' and 'social networking' are ideas that may bridge the gap.

Roman Britain

Candidates will be expected to demonstrate a detailed knowledge of relevant archaeological and literary evidence.

Themes

- Hadrian's Wall – its purpose and main features
- the Roman army in Britain
- Roman towns and buildings
- Roman villas
- Boudicca and Caraticus

Contexts

- archaeological sites and finds as evidence for life in Roman Britain
- the Boudiccan rebellion
- Roman attitudes towards Britain
- the continuing influence of Roman Britain on later times and the similarities and differences between Roman Britain and Britain today

Specimen essay titles

EITHER

- Using evidence from a Roman villa, explain why the Romans developed villas in Britain.

OR

- Do you think that history should look back on Boudicca's rebellion as a success or a failure?

Why choose this option?

This option offers a whole variety of aspects, but is clearly ideal for students with a particular interest in British history, four hundred years of which were spent under Roman rule. Both Boudicca and Caractacus offer exciting examples of early British resistance to Roman rule. It is also an option which allows students access to the original texts, since there are a variety of Roman writers who have left important information about various aspects of the Roman presence in Britain. However, in addition, the option also gives students the opportunity to analyse archaeological evidence, and possibly even visit sites in Britain such as Bath, Chester or Hadrian's Wall.

The option ties in neatly with the other two Roman options in the specification – Rome and Pompeii; the former concentrates on the key elements on Roman civilisation, the latter on life in a typical Roman town. Roman Britain has the advantage of offering students a look at how the Romans exported their civilisation to other parts of the world, and what happened when they came up against other peoples who resisted them. However, this option is also distinct from the other two in that it gives the opportunity to focus on the structure and workings of the Roman army, which will no doubt be of great interest to some of your students.

Key resources

Of course, one of the major assets of the Roman Britain option is that there are some key resources on your doorstep. Depending on where your school is based in the UK, you might be able to organise day or residential trips to sites such as Bath, Chester, Hadrian's Wall, Fishbourne palace or Lullingstone Roman villa. In addition, the Museum of London does excellent organised tours for schools. All of these sites produce very detailed and helpful education packs for teachers and students; it would be worth contacting them and asking for one even if you are not able to visit in person.

From a teacher's perspective, it is a good idea to read a translation of Tacitus' *Agricola*. The Roman historian wrote this about his father in law, Agricola, who was a dynamic and important governor of Roman Britain. For a general reader for both teachers and students, *Roman Britain* by Stephen Hill and Stanley Ireland (Duckworth) is very thorough and has a chapter on Britain before the Romans. *In Search of the Romans* (to be published by Duckworth in 2011) by James Renshaw will cover the material for this specification. On the internet, there is plenty of useful information at **http://www.roman-britain.org/main.htm**, while the BBC website has some very useful resources at **http://www.bbc.co.uk/history/ancient/romans**. The website **http://vindolanda.csad.ox.ac.uk/index.shtml** shows each of the Vindolanda tablets and gives an English translation.

Teaching suggestions

- As already mentioned, it is a great idea to organise a visit to a famous Roman British site – suggested sites are listed above and their websites can easily be found on the internet. In addition, you could also encourage students to research the history of the Romans in Britain in your local area if you live in a part of the country which was colonised.
- If your students are interested in the 'Scots' (then known as 'Picts') and their resistance to the Romans, then the historian Tacitus in his biography of Agricola (chapters 29–38) describes a seminal battle at a place called Mons Groupies' (which has never been satisfactorily identified); his narrative gives a speech to a Pictish leader called Calgacus, who gives a rallying cry to his men. Although Tacitus could not possibly have known what Calgacus said (there were no translators between the local language and Latin!), it is an interesting attempt by a Roman historian to see the Roman conquest through the eyes of the invaded.
- It is a very good idea to challenge students to think about the pros and cons of the Roman conquest of Britain. Perhaps set up a debate between students, with one representing a Roman, another a pro-Roman Briton, and finally one arguing from the position of a resistance fighter. They should come to see that there are arguments on both sides.
- As with all the topics, there is real scope for the students to write an account of their lives in Roman Britain. A particular area of focus here might be the Vindolanda tablets – ask your students to read about these and then imagine that they too are living on the northern frontier. They could make up their own messages back home (you could give this a modern twist and get them to write emails home).
- Encourage students to reflect on the legacy left by the Romans in Britain today, in the form of roads, towns, place names, language or even landscape.

Appendix 1 List of recordings provided on the CD-ROM

Homer, The Odyssey

Translation by E V Rieu revised D C H Rieu (Penguin Classics, revised edition 1991)

Track 1 Odysseus prepares to leave Calypso (Book 5)
from page 67 line 159 'The goddess came ...'
to page 69 line 246 '... edges straight'

Track 2 Odysseus meets Nausicaa (Book 6)
from page 79 line 110 'When she was about ...'
to page 82 line 238 '... beautiful-haired attendants'

Track 3 Odysseus avoids revealing his identity (Book 7)
from page 90 line 208 'Alcinous ...'
to page 90 line 227 '... talked good sense'

Track 4 Odysseus reveals his identity to Alcinous (Book 9)
from page 110 line 19 'I am Odysseus ...'
to page 111 line 38 '... back from Troy'

Track 5 The Cyclops (Book 9)
from page 115 line 193 'At this point ...'
to page 124 line 565 '... from death'

Track 6 Circe (Book 10)
from page 133 line 307 'Hermes ...'
to page 136 line 444 '... enchanted castle'

Track 7 Scylla (Book 12)
from page 162 line 201 'We had no sooner ...'
to page 163 line 259 '... sight than that'

Track 8 The storm (Book 12)
from page 168 line 425 'The storm that ...'
to page 168 line 446 '... certain death'

Ovid, Metamorphoses

Translation by David Raeburn (Penguin Classics 2004)

Track 9 Deucalion and Pyrrha (Book 1)
from page 25 line 397 'Proceeding down ...'
to page 25 line 415 '... stony origin'

Track 10 Daphne (Book 1)
from page 31 line 530 'Flight made her ...'
to page 33 line 567 '... in the treetop'

Track 11 Io (Book 1)
from page 35 line 588 'As Io was one day ...'
to page 38 line 667 '... in every direction'

Track 12 Cadmus (Book 3)
from page 94 line 28 'Nearby stood an ancient ...'
to page 97 line 100 '... terror'

Track 13 Semele (Book 3)
from page 105 line 260 'Semele, Cadmus' ...'
to page 107 line 315 '... milk'

Track 14 Narcissus and Echo (Book 3)
from page 109 line 339 'Soon ...'
to page 116 line 510 '... petals'

Track 15 Pentheus and Bacchus (Book 3)
from page 126 line 701 'Pentheus remained ...'
to page 127 line 731 '... hands'

Track 16 Scylla (Book 8)
from page 294 line 1 'The morning star ...'
to page 301 line 151 '... the shorn lock'

Track 17 Daedalus and Icarus (Book 8)
from page 303 line 183 'Daedalus now had ...'
to page 305 line 235 '... Icaria'

Track 18 Meleäger (Book 8)
from page 312 line 371 'Now Castor ...'
to page 315 line 444 '... the other's'

Track 19 Althaea (Book 8)
from page 318 line 499 'Oh, where ...'
to page 319 line 525 '... embers'

Track 20 Philemon and Baucis (Book 8)
from page 327 line 690 'You alone ...'
to page 328 line 724 '... worshipped'

Track 21 Erysichthon (Book 8)
from page 329 line 741 'He, as the story goes ...'
to page 332 line 808 '... excrescence'

Appendix 2 Tyrtaios (Diehl³ 1.1.9)

'I would not remember nor include in my song any man for swiftness of foot or wrestling skill, not even if he had the strength and stature of the Cyclops and ran more swiftly than the north wind from Thrace, not yet if he were more handsome than Tithonus or wealthier than Midas or Cinyras, nor again if he were more royal than Pelops the son of Tantalus or more sweet-tongued than Adrastus, nor even if he had every virtue other than might in war. A man is not good in war unless he has the courage to look on blood and slaughter and stand face to face with his foe and strike. This is virtue, this is the best and finest prize for a young man to win among men. It is a blessing common to the city and the whole people when a man stands firm in the front rank with determination, utterly forgetting the disgrace of flight, protected by his courage and endurance, steeling his neighbour by his words; this man is good in war. Swiftly he routs the savage ranks of the enemy, eagerly he stems the tide of battle. He who falls in the front rank and loses his dear life brings glory to his country, his people and his father; wounded many times in front through shield and breastplate, he is mourned by old and young alike, and the whole city grieves with bitter longing. His tomb, his children and his line are marked out among men; never will his glory and his fame perish; although he is in the tomb, he achieves immortality, for mighty Ares slew him at his moment of glory as he stood and fought for his children and his land. If he escapes the black fate of death and upholds the proud boast of his spear in victory, young and old alike honour him, and great are his joys before he dies; as he grows old he is outstanding among the citizens and none would willingly deprive him of his honour or his rights; all yield place to him, the young, his contemporaries and his elders. This is the peak of virtue to which each should now aspire, never relaxing in war.' (Diehl³ 1.1.9)

Handout 1 Sample essay response (high level): Epic and Myth option 2 (Ovid, Metamorphoses)

Read the essay question, student response and examiner comments below. Annotate the essay to show evidence for the comments provided by the examiner.

Is the moral of the *Metamorphoses* simply that bad behaviour is always punished?

If we examine a sample of the Metamorphoses, we can assess whether Ovid is giving us a straightforward message that people are made to suffer because of their crimes, or whether the moral is more complicated than that.

There is no doubt but that some characters are punished for bad behaviour. In reality however the bad behaviour seems more to do with divine vanity than actual sin in its human context.

In Book 1 Lycaon has committed a crime against Jupiter by mocking the people's piety and serving up a hostage for dinner. Jupiter destroys his palace with lightning and turns him into a wolf. Jupiter then goes on to punish the whole earth for its bad behaviour by sending a flood. A similar message is given in Book 8 where Erysichthon insists on cutting down a tree which is sacred to Ceres even when the poor tree is crying out. When Ceres punishes him for his crime by making him constantly hungry, and he is reduced to consuming his own limbs, we feel that the moral is that his bad behaviour has been punished. This particular story treats the killing of the slave as almost incidental. Ceres punishes Erysicthon because of his treatment of her tree.

The moral at this stage seems very clear: irrespective of other forms of bad behaviour it is a person's treatment of the gods which really counts. This is further reinforced by the story of the wild boar which Diana sends to the land of Aetolia because the people forget to worship her.

Once again the people's behaviour is not really bad, it is more a case of the goddess being offended just because she is not being worshipped.

Pentheus, too is punished just for offending a god. He refuses to worship Dionysus and the god makes his mother tear him apart, thinking she has captured a boar.

In fact we may take this even further and say that sometimes punishments are dished out when people offend the gods through no fault of their own. There are numerous examples of this:

Cadmus and his family were punished by Juno just because they were the family of Europa who, through no fault of her own was abducted by Jupiter.

Semele was blasted by the sight of Jupiter, and Echo deprived of speech, by a jealous Juno. They were punished, but their behaviour, though it annoyed Juno was not really bad.

Similarly, Actaeon saw Diana naked, but by accident, and was torn apart by his own dogs as punishment. Ovid even adds that some people thought that the goddess had gone too far in her revenge. This is not a case of just punishment, but cruel revenge.

Sometimes suffering seems random rather than a consequence of bad behaviour:

Narcissus is turned into a flower because of his vanity – he pays no attention to any of his admirers and loves only his own reflection. This is in a sense a punishment for his behaviour, but as he was destined to suffer when he knew himself, there is the idea that he was not totally to blame for his punishment.

Despite the overwhelming evidence therefore that the moral is that the gods are to be feared or else, there are examples where the gods do judge people by their character rather than just their piety.

Deucalion and Pyrrha are saved by Jupiter from the flood because of their great piety. Philomen and Baucis are the only people to offer hospitality to Jupiter and Mercury, serving their best food and even trying to kill their goose for the gods. It is important to acknowledge that they did not know that they were gods then and were recognised for their natural hospitality and kindness. They thus watch everyone else being destroyed as punishment, whilst they are granted their wish to die together and become eternal companions in the form of an oak and a linden.

Some stories do have a natural sense of justice where, irrespective of the gods, bad behaviour gains its just reward. Scylla betrays her father by cutting off his lock, and the last we see of her she has been turned into a small bird and is being pursued by her father in the form of a bird of prey, punished for her crime.

The moral message of the Metamorphoses therefore is rather more complicated than just being a case of bad behaviour always being punished. A more clear moral might be that, despite all else, man should avoid offending the gods at all costs as this guarantees punishment and there is always a chance that a person's bad behaviour will be punished. On the positive side, though, genuine goodness will be rewarded.

And so, although it is true that many characters are punished as a direct result of their bad behaviour, this does not apply to others who are punished unfairly or who are rewarded for good behaviour, and so the moral is not as simple as 'bad behaviour is always punished'.

Examiner comments

AO1 Thorough knowledge – a wide range of relevant stories used, with accurate detail and good overview, clearly expressed. 11/11

AO2 Thorough understanding of the reasons for the punishments – distinguishes between types and explains the nature of the punishment. 7/8

AO3 Follows the argument and evaluates the truth of the essay title thoroughly for each example. Could have given a broader overview of stories not associated with piety – do the majority of tales have a moral? 10/11

Total 28/30

Handout 2 Sample essay response (mid level): Epic and Myth option 2 (Ovid, Metamorphoses)

Read the essay question, student response and examiner comments below. Annotate the essay to show evidence for the comments provided by the examiner.

> Is the moral of the *Metamorphoses* simply that bad behaviour is always punished?

In the metamophoses bad behaviour is always punished.

One very good example of this is the story of Erysichton. There is an oak tree growing on his land that is sacred to Ceres and where the dyrad's dance. He orders it to be cut down with an axe, and hits it, saying that he doesn't care. Even when the tree groans and blood pours from the trunk, he carries on. He hears a voice from the tree which tells him he will be punished Ceres sends Hunger to him and after hunger has gone to him in the night and breathed in him he suffers all the time because he is always hungry no matter how much he has eaten and then he has nothing left because he has spent all his money on food. The only thing he has left is his daughter and he decides to sell her so he can buy more food but she is clever and can change herself and so when someone has bought her she changes and then goes back to her father and is sold again. In the end he is so hungry that he starts to eat himself.

Pentheus behaves badly and he is punished as well. He would not wership the god Dionysiss and when he goes to the mountain to spy on the women who have all gone their his mother Agave sees him and thinks he is a wild boar. She and the women chase him screaming and shouting and they pull his arms off and his legs and his mother pulls off his head and there is blood everywhere on the mountain and all over his mother and the other women.

Narcissus is punished because he is turned into a flower. He was very big headed and even though lots of girls thought he was really cool he just ignored them. One day Echoe saw him and fell in love with him. She followed him around but she couldn't speak to him properly because all she could say was the last words that she had heard someone else say and so she repeated what he said. She followed him everywhere but because he told her to get lost she went and hid in a cave and her skin went all dry and she shrivelled and died and all that was left was her bones and voice, and then her bones were turned to stone and so there was only her voice. Narcissus carried on annoying everyone with his ways, and someone prayed that he would fall in love but never get love in return. This came true because when he went to a pond and bent down to have a drink he saw a person in the water and fell in love. He did not know that it was his own reflection and so did not understand why it would not answer him and why it kept disappearing when he tried to touch it. He got very upset and he loved the face in the water so much that he stayed looking at it all the time. He did not eat or drink or sleep but just got upset about the reflection and in the end he died.

Where he had died a yellow flower grew on the spot where he had died and nobody could find his body. And so he was punished for being so in love with himself.

Acteaon was punished too because he saw the goddess Diana in the nude. She was angry with him because humans shouldn't see naked goddesses. She punishes him in a very violent way. She turns him into a deer and then his hunting dogs see him and attack him. He runs away and wants to shout at them to tell them who he is, but he can't because he is an animal and can't speak. They put their teeth in his back and neck and all over until he is torn apart and dead. He really was punished for his bad behaviour seeing Diana with no clothes on.

Therefore it is true that the moral of the metamophoses is that people are punished for their bad behaviour.

Examiner comments

AO1 Demonstrates sound knowledge of the text, based on a range of relevant stories. Meaning is communicated clearly, but there are some weaknesses in English. 7/11

AO2 Demonstrates some understanding, but does not distinguish between bad behaviour being punished and bad luck/innocent mistakes leading to punishment. 4/8

AO3 Some analysis of evidence, but tends to include too much narrative. No consideration of whether the proposition in the title is, in fact, untrue. 5/11

Total 16/30

Handout 3 Sample essay response (high level): City Life in the Classical World option 1 (Athens)

Read the essay question, student response and examiner comments below. Annotate the essay to show evidence for the comments provided by the examiner.

Explain to what extent theatre was an important part of Athenian life.

We can still see in Athens today the theatre of Dionysos which held more than 15,000 people. The size tells us that it must have been very important. There are also many pictures of actors on Greek vases, another indication of its popularity.

One reason the theatre was important is that the City Dionysia, the main drama festival, provided a five-day holiday in the spring, starting with a torchlight procession when the statue of Dionysos was led into the theatre. The next day there was another grand procession, with drinking and revels going on until late in the evening, and then three days of plays followed by the results day. The comedy festival, the Lenaia, gave citizens a break and an opportunity to drink and laugh during the cold infertile winter. There were no weekends in ancient Athens, and so these enjoyable festivals must have been very welcome.

Fertility was a real concern for the ancient Athenians. They needed their crops to grow and to produce sons, and so to worship the god of wine and fertility, Dionysos, was important. The priest of Dionysus had a special seat at the theatre , and there was an altar to the god in the middle of the orchestra. The chorus sang hymns to the gods throughout the plays. This religious aspect of the theatre makes it very much part of people's lives.

The theatre was also important because it provided good entertainment. Satyr plays contained amusing, animal-like figures behaving wildly. In the comedies the chorus might be dressed as frogs or wasps, and there would be farce, puns and rude jokes. In tragedies there were dramatic stories such as that of Oedipus, who blinded himself when he realised that he had killed his father and married his mother, or Agamemnon whose wife Clytemnestra murdered him when he returned from Troy. The opportunity to see such things would have been very important to the Athenians, because they didn't have all the technology we have for entertainment.

The fact that the drama festival was a competition made it more important. The audience would be eager to see what fantastic things the playwright had thought up to get votes, such as a spectacular use of the mekhane to bring on a snake-drawn chariot, or the ekkuklema piled up high with bodies. They might have a favourite playwright such as Aeschylus, Sophocles or Euripides, or want a particular actor or choregos to win. The judges were members of the tribes, and that would add excitement because they would feel that they were involved in the decision.

As the theatre was a good way of communicating with all the population in a world without the mass media of today, it was an important way of getting over messages. In Oedipus, for example, the moral message is that man should not be proud and arrogant, but should always honour the gods. The comedies of Aristophanes were political satire and the behaviour of politicians such as Cleon, wrong decisions by people in the ekklesia and events in the war with Sparta were among the things laughed at and criticised.

The theatre in Athens had a political role. At the City Dionysia, the Greek states who paid tribute to Athens handed over the money in the theatre, and the theatre was also the place where the orphans of men killed in battle were paraded. This shows that it was important for propaganda reasons and would make the Athenians feel very proud of themselves.

And so the theatre was very important in the lives of the Athenians because of its religious, political and moral nature as well as the great entertainment it provided.

Examiner comments

AO1 Very thorough knowledge based on full range of relevant factual information. Detailed overview. Full of accurate detail, including reference to specific plays (although these are not required). 11/11

AO2 Understands Athenian context of theatre and explains clearly the implications of the evidence. Could have discussed composition of audience. 7/8

AO3 Responds well to question, good personal response. Essay progresses to a logical conclusion.

11/11

Total 29/30

Handout 4 Sample essay response (mid level): City Life in the Classical World option 1 (Athens)

Read the essay question, student response and examiner comments below. Annotate the essay to show evidence for the comments provided by the examiner.

Explain to what extent theatre was an important part of Athenian life.

The theatres in Athens were absolutely huge, and so lots of people must have gone to them and it must have been very important. When they were all at the theatre normal life in Athens must have stopped.

The theatres were open-air and there was no electricity and so only natural light was available. This meant that the plays were during the day and they went on all day. If the plays went on all day and the theatres were full, then that tells me that people must have taken a day's holiday to go the theatre. I don't suppose they would have taken days off work unless what they were going to see was really important to them.

The Greek theatre was important it was linked to religion and there was an altar in the middle of the theatre. In Athens people must have taken the theatre seriously and the fact that it was partly religious must have made them take much more notice of the messages in the plays. The chorus used to sing to the gods, and so going to the theatre might have been a bit like going to church for us, and would have been very important to people who were religious.

Greek tragedies were about death and murder in families, which shows that this subject was important to the Greeks. Today we have stories about those things in soaps like EastEnders, and I suppose the ancient Greeks liked exciting storylines like we do. They couldn't watch them very often though, so it must have been very exciting for them when there was the chance to watch a tragedy. They had comedies too, a bit like pantomimes, where actors wore masks and made fun of people. They didn't have radio or newspapers, but the theatre let them have a good laugh at there politicians which was an important way they could say what they thought.

Greek drama was part of an important competition. I suppose that watching a drama competition live in the big theatre with the whole population must have been brilliant for the Athenians and something they would look forward to every year, a bit like we enjoy watching the Oscars on television or the Eurovision song contest.

The Greek theatre was not just about acting, there was singing too and going to the theatre meant listening to the chorus. This made the theatre an important occasion for the Greeks because they wouldn't have been able to listen to music like we can because they had only live music.

There was no radio or television in the ancient world, and so the Greek theatre must have been the only time when it was possible to speak to thousands of people at the same time. We have broadcasts and documentaries to tell people important messages, about politics and behaviour. The Greeks could use the theatre to tell people important things about politicians and wars and how they should worship the gods. It was obviously very important because of this.

The theatre was important to the Athenians. We know this because they liked to show it off to visitors to Athens who were invited to the festival so they could admire Athens and see how clever and wealthy the citizens were.

I think that their theatre was much more important to the ancient Athenians than ours is to us today.

Examiner comments

AO1 Some knowledge of the theatre implied, but very little fact or evidence here. 4/11

AO2 Some understanding and explanation of the role of the theatre in the ancient context. 4/8

AO3 Some very good personal response and perceptive observations despite the lack of fact. In terms of evaluation, a sound piece of work. Though not required, the candidate has made a good effort to use modern comparisons to illustrate his points. 8/11

Total 16/30